Not Not Not Not
Not Enough Oxygen
and Other Plays

Caryl Churchill

Not Not Not Not Not Enough Oxygen

and Other Plays

edited by
Terry Gifford and Gill Round

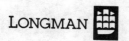

First published 1993

Set in 10/12 point Baskerville, Linotron 202
Produced by Longman Singapore Publishers (Pte) Ltd
Printed in Singapore

ISBN 0 582 08297 8

EG05892

Acknowledgements   822·92

We are indebted to the Editor and Geraldine Cousin for
permission to include extracts from an interview with Caryl
Churchill from *New Theatre Quarterly* IV, 13, Feb. 1988
(Cambridge University Press).

Contents

Contents

Introduction

Caryl Churchill on her work

Below are extracts from interviews with Caryl Churchill where she has talked about different aspects of her writing.

On beginning writing

I believe you began writing as a child? Was it plays or stories?

Stories and poems. I wrote one very short play once. When I was about fourteen, I wrote a full-length children's pony book; just the kind of thing I'd stopped enjoying reading myself. That gave me a huge feeling of achievement, to have something completed and of that length.

Did you know at that age that you wanted to be a writer?

Yes, I can remember consciously thinking of it from when I was about eight.

Did you begin to write because of a love of words, do you think?

I don't know. That must be part of it. The fact that I was an only child may have helped. I had friends, but I did have quite a lot of time when I could be alone. Planning stories would be like solitary playing. I would invent a lot of characters, and descriptions of where they lived and maps, and it would be a whole game. So there was that sort of overlap. I also had a very close friend and we used to play a game which, looking back, reached a point where it was more like improvising plays. We would work out in some detail what was going to happen and we would play it, and, if we hadn't quite liked how it went, we would play it again. So, it began to merge in *that* way. But I just wrote a lot, and I was also separately interested in the theatre. I liked going to plays. I used to want there to be plays done at school, and there weren't. When I was fifteen, I went off to a summer theatre in Canada, outside Montreal, and painted scenery. I didn't really put the two things together till a few years after that, at university.

(Interview with Geraldine Cousin, *New Theatre Quarterly*, IV, 13, February 1988)

On writing for radio

The first play that you had performed professionally (on radio) was The Ants?

Professionally, yes.

You didn't really intend it for radio, did you?

No, I thought of it as a television play. I hadn't realised, I think, what a visual medium radio is at that point.

You went on to write a number of plays for radio. Did you choose to write for radio for pragmatic reasons, or was it also fascination with the medium?

I think it was both, because I listened to radio a lot. As a child, I was of a generation who grew up with radio, not television. Television was around at the end of my childhood, but I don't remember it ever being important at all. Radio was, and it was nice because you could do other things at the same time, like drawing. I went on listening to radio, Beckett plays, for example. Until, I suppose, my early twenties radio was really quite important to me. So it was partly that, and partly having had one radio play done.

(Interview with Geraldine Cousin, *New Theatre Quarterly*, IV, 13, February 1988)

[I went on writing short plays for radio] partly because [I liked radio but also because] I began having children . . . There was also a better market for them. It was very different, in the early sixties. There wasn't anywhere near the number of fringe and lunchtime theatres, and the radio was an accessible way of having your plays done. . . . If your play was seventeen minutes long, they wouldn't ask you to make it thirteen. . . .

[In the radio plays] I focused on the the awfulness of everything rather than on the possibilities for change.

(Interview with Judith Thurman, 'Caryl Churchill: the Playwright Who Makes You Laugh', *Ms*, May 1982)

Radio is good because it makes you . . . precise . . . Then there's the freedom – you can do almost anything in a radio play, whereas you're tied to the possibilities of the set and the stage in the theatre. I think in those days I was more concerned with words, and less with events, though . . . I feel I'm better at managing events now. . . .

I . . . reached the point of finding it hard to make people speak to each other – there would simply be monologues delivered, say, by one twin and then the other. I felt this . . . Becketty thing happening: . . . I was going to finish up with a play that was two words and a long silence. Then things began to get better. These plays weren't necessarily depressing: some were fairly funny, but they had to do in some way with difficulties of being.

(Interview with John Hall, 'Close Up', *The Guardian*, 12 December 1972)

On political theatre

Does the playwright have an obligation to take a moral and political stance?

It's almost impossible not to take one, whether you intend to or not. Most plays can be looked at from a political perspective and have said something, even if it isn't what you set out to say.

If you wrote a West End comedy relying on conventional sexist jokes, that's taking a moral and political stance, though the person who wrote it might say, 'I was just writing an entertaining show'. Whatever you do your point of view is going to show somewhere. It usually only gets noticed and called 'political' if it's against the *status quo*. There are times when I feel I want to deal with immediate issues and times when I don't. I do like the stuff of theatre, in the same way that people who are painting like paint; and of course when you say 'moral and political' that doesn't have to imply reaching people logically or overtly, because theatre can reach people on all kinds of other levels too.... Sometimes it's going to be about images, more like a dream to people, and sometimes it's going to be more like reading an article.

(Interview with Kathleen Betsko and Rachel Koenig, *Interviews with Contemporary Women Playwrights*, Beach Tree Books, New York, 1987)

I've constantly said that I am both a socialist and a feminist. Constantly said it. If someone says a 'socialist playwright' or a 'feminist playwright' that can suggest to some people something rather narrow which doesn't cover as many things as you might be thinking about. I get asked if I mind being called a woman playwright or a feminist playwright, and again it depends entirely on what's going on in the mind of the person who says it.

(Interview with Linda Fitzsimmons, 21 April 1988, *File on Churchill* , compiled by Linda Fitzsimmons, Methuen, 1989)

On being 'a woman writer'

In the radio plays, the main voice is frequently male. Most of the characters in Vinegar Tom *and* Fen *are women, and in* Top Girls *they're all women.* Softcops *has an all male cast. Are you conscious of exploring different gender-based ideas at any one particular time?*

I think originally I wasn't really interested in gender ideas at all. I probably made main characters men without thinking of it consciously at all, but just because main characters tended to *be* men. It was also perhaps easier to conceive of characters separate from myself by making them men. To an extent, I was at that point in a slightly conscious reaction from the kind of semi-autobiographical novels that quite a lot of women of my generation were starting to write – Françoise Sagan, for example, and Margaret Drabble. That seemed to be something I definitely didn't want to do. I wanted to make something more distanced. Then I became increasingly interested in women's issues and consciously chose to write about those. *Softcops* being all men just came from the material. It would have been almost contrived to have included women because of what the play's about, a system of power operated by men. Now . . . once you've become conscious of gender, it's hard not to be always aware of what gender you've chosen for a character.

Do you think of yourself not just as a writer, but as 'a woman writer'?

Sometimes. Originally, not. During the seventies there was a context for thinking of myself as a woman writer. Other people were thinking of me in that way and I was becoming more interested in women's issues. I became more aware of myself then as a woman writer. I think it's one of those things that you can feel completely differently about depending on the context. I remember *way* back somebody writing about one of my radio plays, and saying that you wouldn't know it had been written by a woman. The writer clearly meant this as praise, and that gave me pause. Most of the time I didn't think about it, but there were little moments of realisation. If, for example, a critic refers to you as one of the best women writers, and you feel there's any possibility that he thinks of that as a *lesser* category, you resent the use of it as a term. If it means women themselves thinking about things that they haven't thought about before, then you can actually feel very positive about the idea of being a woman writer, and obviously this is attractive and powerful. Most of the time I don't think about it either way, really.

You don't see a woman writer's job as being different in our society from a man writer's?

I do sometimes. I think I feel quite differently at different times about writing. I'm only just beginning to realise that it is alright to be inconsistent. There are times when I'm aware of things . . . and at other times they're not on my mind.

(Interview with Geraldine Cousin, *New Theatre Quarterly*, IV, 13, February 1988)

Has the political climate for women dramatists changed drastically since you began writing plays?

I began writing plays in 1958, and I don't think I knew any other women playwrights then. Luckily, I didn't think about it. . . . [Tillie Olsen in *Silences*] says that at different times, whole categories of people are enabled to write. You tend to think of your own development only having to do with yourself and it's exciting to discover it in a historical context.

(Interview with Kathleen Betsko and Rachel Koenig, *Interviews with Contemporary Women Playwrights*, Beech Tree Books, New York, 1987)

Women are traditionally expected not to initiate action, and plays are action, in a way that words are not. So perhaps that's one reason why comparatively few women have written plays.

(Interview with Linda Fitzsimmons, 21 April 1988, *File on Churchill*, compiled by Linda Fitzsimmons, Methuen, 1989)

On writing comedy

How much do you aim for comic effects?
I don't think I set out to be funny. Things that end up being serious or being funny I usually set about in exactly the same way. And it isn't really clear which it's going to be until I'm quite far on into the material.
(Interview with Lynne Truss, *Plays and Players*, January 1984)

About the playwright

Caryl Churchill was born in London on 3 September 1938, the only child of a cartoonist and a fashion model. When she was ten, the family moved to Montreal, Canada. 'It was there I began writing short stories and producing living-room panto-mimes,' she recalls. 'I wrote constantly.' She remembers making up plays with a friend and acting them out together. This ordinary 'playing' at making plays for fun as a child was the beginning of a process which has led to Caryl Churchill being described by the theatre director, Max Stafford-Clark, as 'Britain's finest living playwright'. What is perhaps less ordinary is that she had written a full-length story about children and ponies by the time she was fourteen. This pushing herself to have finished something, she regards as important for her future writing.

The story of Caryl Churchill's career as a writer is a combination of an extraordinary imagination, persistence and a refusal to be satisfied with easy answers. She returned to Britain from Montreal in 1957 to become a student at Lady Margaret Hall, Oxford. Here she wrote *Downstairs*, which won first prize at the *Sunday Times*/National Union of Students Drama Festival. Even at this time Caryl Churchill was experimenting with dramatic form. She wrote a radio play and two other stage plays which were produced by students, one of which was in verse, while the other included songs. All three plays also tried out the use of a narrator and unusual ways of presenting the action through stylised rather than naturalistic acting.

A year after leaving university, Caryl Churchill married and over the next few years had three children. In 1962 the first professional production of one of her plays was broadcast on the radio. During this period she decided to concentrate on writing short plays for radio because it enabled her to combine writing with caring for very young children. Following the broadcast in 1967 of *Not Not Not Not Not Enough Oxygen* the reviewer in *The Listener* said 'Caryl Churchill is a writer with an obvious talent for the medium'.

The Judge's Wife, the first of her plays to be produced on television, was written at about the same time as *Not Not Not Not Not Enough Oxygen* and shown on BBC 2 in 1972. One reviewer wrote:

> *The Judge's Wife* was one of those plays which leaves the critic with a strong sense of frustration; seeing so much originality just failing in the event to fulfil its promise.

Although now well-established as a radio playwright, Caryl Churchill had not stopped writing for the theatre, and in 1972 her first professionally produced stage play was performed at the Royal Court Theatre. This theatre was the first to recognise her talent and gave her a job as resident playwright for a year in 1974.

In 1976 Caryl Churchill first worked with Joint Stock Theatre Group and with one of its founding directors, Max Stafford-Clark. The play was *Light Shining in Buckinghamshire*, a historical play about the possibilities for freedom after the king had been defeated in the Civil War of the seventeenth century.

Joint Stock has developed a particular way of working. Actors, director and writer all explore the theme of the play together, researching 'not just information', Caryl Churchill says, 'but your attitudes to it, and possible ways of showing things'. The writer still goes away and writes the play, in a twelve-week gap between the research period and rehearsal. Caryl Churchill describes this from a writer's point of view:

> If you're working by yourself then you're not accountable to anyone but yourself while you're doing it. You don't get forced in quite the same way into seeing how your inner feelings connect up with larger things that happen to other people.

Later work with Joint Stock produced *Cloud Nine* in 1979, a play about sexual confusions. In 1982 the company stayed together in an East Anglian village to research *Fen*, a play about women farm workers. By 1980 Max Stafford-Clark had been appointed director of the Royal Court Theatre and he brought with him his interest in this way of working. Two years later he directed *Top Girls*, a play about the costs to women of being 'successful' in Mrs Thatcher's Britain. In 1986 Stafford-Clark asked Caryl Churchill to research a play about the City of London; *Serious Money* was the result. It won several awards and was eventually produced in the West End of London and on Broadway in New York.

Even before *Serious Money*, Caryl Churchill's plays were being produced in many different countries, from Australia to Brazil, and from Japan to Iceland. Nevertheless, she continues to pursue what is interesting rather than what is commercially popular. In 1990 she went to Romania with a group of drama students to make a play, *Mad Forest*, about life before and after the reign of the Communist dictator Ceauşescu. Caryl Churchill says:

> The only point of working is to do the kind of work you want to do. Obviously money comes into it, but I'm so used to not making any that I don't seek ways of getting it. It's a bit like playing a fruit machine. Sometimes, suddenly, it pours out lots, but most of the time I'm pulling madly at the handle and nothing comes out.

Caryl Churchill has always taken risks in her plays by exploring commonplace tensions in imaginative and often unconventional ways. In some plays, for example, women are played by men, and men's roles played by women. Sometimes several people speak at once (as they do in real life). Historical characters can appear in discussion with modern characters. The scene can shift to a quite different reality in order to compare experiences in different situations. As a result some people have initially found her plays puzzling, whilst others have found that they immediately shed new light on old problems such as sexism and racism. None of the three early plays in this book shows Caryl Churchill at her most unconventional as a dramatist, but each play is unusual in different ways: *Seagulls* explores the problems raised as a consequence of a 'housewife' discovering that she has an extraordinary ability; *Not Not Not Not Not Enough Oxygen* is set in the year 2010 in a place called 'the Londons'; *The Judge's Wife* is a television play which begins by showing the murder of a judge and then explores the build-up to the murder before giving the judge's wife a surprising closing speech.

Caryl Churchill has recalled a moment when

...I thought, 'Wait a minute, my whole concept of what a play might be is from plays written by men...' And I remember long before that thinking of the 'maleness' of the traditional structure of plays, with conflict and building in a certain way to a climax.

Her own 'concept of what a play might be' has developed rather differently. Rather than conflict, her plays are based on the interaction between people and their ideas. Rather than ending with a climax her plays leave the audience with a much more open-ended invitation to decide for themselves what they think has really been happening and what the outcome of the action might be. This is what makes her plays so interesting to discuss. They need an audience to decide what they mean.

How to read plays

None of these three plays by Caryl Churchill was written to be read as a text. Each was written to be experienced in a very different way. *Seagulls* is a script to be produced by a director and actors for a live theatre audience. *Not Not Not Not Not Enough Oxygen* was intended for an audience who could only hear what was happening in the play – a radio audience; and the director of *The Judge's Wife* would be using the script in this book to create for the television audience the series of talking pictures Caryl Churchill wants her audience to experience.

These three types of play each make the audience's imagination work in different ways. So while you are reading each one, you have to think about the way an audience would be experiencing it. Similarly, when putting on a production, the director of each play has to think about this and plan accordingly: there will be lots of decisions to make about how to present the script and the director will need to make notes on each page.

To help you think about how these decisions may differ in different contexts, the first page of each script is annotated with examples of an imaginary director's notes on how to use the different media – live theatre, radio and television – to set the scene and stimulate an audience's imagination. Of course, other directors, or the writer herself, might want to create quite different effects from these play-texts and would make different notes in their margins.

Seagulls – *a stage play*

Characters

VALERY, middle-aged   *plain, slow speaking*
DI, slightly younger   *ambitious, pushy*
CLIFF, young, American   *keen, enthusiastic*

Green grass, clear sky.   **The stage set should slope up to sky.**
                           Park. Flower bed stage left.

VALERY *and* DI.   *sitting on grass stage right*

DI *looks at her watch.*   *nervous, facing audience*

VALERY   I don't like it.   *back to audience*

DI   What? What don't you like?   *slightly jumpy*

VALERY   Can we get tea?

DI   And cakes. I told them you'd like cakes.

VALERY   I don't like the open air.   *looking around towards*
                                      audience

DI   It's only for charity.

VALERY   I don't eat cakes before.   *emphasis*

DI   You do.

VALERY   I don't any more.

DI   You still drink tea?

VALERY   What tea?   *distracted. Looking away still*

DI   You can eat the cakes after.   *pause*

VALERY   Yes I can, you are lovely Di, I'm
   sorry I'm so nasty, I'm not in the mood

today. I wish we were just here with nothing to do like everyone else. I wish I'd come to see somebody else do something wonderful instead of being the one. *looks at Di for the first time*

DI   You enjoy it.

VALERY   You don't have to do anything. *pause*

DI *looks at her watch.*

DI   We've nothing on the whole of next week except packing and I'll do all that. We can go and watch other people every day. What would you like? We could go to a concert. *encouraging*

VALERY   You know I hate concerts. *irritated at Di*

Not Not Not Not Not Enough Oxygen – *a radio play*

nervously fast; pause at full stops

VIVIAN   Shall I tell you what I bought today? Not enough enough oxygen in this block, why always headache. Spoke caretaker, caretaker says speak manager, manager says local authority local authority won't give us won't give us the money. Said I said what's the no point giving us faster – all be dead corpses in the faster lifts if there's not not not not not enough oxygen. Caretaker caretaker said his part his personal if it was up to if it was down to him would put big plants big plants plants *slightly whining voice; London accent pretending to be posh*

plants in every room. Do stop walking
about Mick. Mick do keep still as if you
were paying as if you were hearing me.

pause

MICK   I'm waiting for my son.

*strong London accent;
deep voice (aged 60)*

VIVIAN   Listen, it will take your mind take
your mind off. What I said plants plants
would take money. Earth plants earth
would all have to come in from the park
and the park the park authority the park
authority wouldn't permit. Because hardly
any park hardly any park left. My sister
told me she went went went went to, four
days four days days days to get and the
crowd was the crowd was the crowd was
just like home.

caring

MICK   How late will he be?

VIVIAN   The grass can only – Mick why not
go up on the roof and walk about walk
about about in the haze? There's no room
in this room in this room. You take five
five steps remind that mad cat cat in cage
at the zoo up and up and down up and –

*getting
annoyed
pause*

He sits down.

Yes sit do sit and breathe quietly. Breathe
quietly. It was Claude's own it was Claude
said his own idea to come so he will. Shall
we do some more of the big jig big jigsaw?

calming

MICK *pays no attention.*   *long silence*

The Judge's Wife – *a TV play*

This is a storyboard for the opening shots.

1 Judge lies dead in wood.		Medium shot. Still. Must recognise Judge in next shot. *No sound.*
2 Judge and Michael Warren standing in wood.		Long shot. Michael Warren is talking quietly. *No sound.*
3 Warren shoots Judge.		Long shot. Zoom as Warren pulls gun to medium shot. Judge falls. *Sound from shot onwards.*
4 As in 1.		As in 1. *Continue word/sound.*
5 Cut to car entering wood. Stops at edge.		Long shot of car coming towards camera, passing, stopping in medium shot. *Sound.*
6 Judge and Warren get out. Walk into wood.		Medium shot. Pan with them until they disappear into trees. *Continue sound.*

7	As in 2.		As in 2. *Sound.*
8	As in 3.		As in 3. *Sound.*
9	As in 1.		As in 1. *Sound.*
10	Judge looking down. Looks up. Speaks.		Close-up. *Sound.*

How to write plays

Your reading of these plays will be helped if you write plays for live theatre, radio and television audiences. Several of the Coursework assignments on pages 67–81 invite you to write for these three different kinds of audiences. It might be helpful to remind you of the conventions for setting out plays.

Setting out a stage play

Make a cast list for the first scene, then add to it as you bring in new characters. Give the director some notes on the age and appearance of each character. Give the actor some notes about the character's relationship or attitude to the other characters.

- Describe the time and place of the general setting at the beginning of each scene (e.g. The present. 6 p.m. A park).
- Describe what you want the audience to see on stage (e.g. *Seagulls*: 'Green grass, clear sky').
- Make a rough plan of the number of scenes, the location of each and the key plot events in each.
- Put your stage directions in brackets when you want to tell the actors when there is a crucial action.
- Put the name of each character in the left margin (e.g. next to the words they speak).
- Write your first draft on alternate lines of your paper so that you have space for revisions.

Setting out a radio play

- 'SFX' is an abbreviation for Sound Effects. Put SFX in the margin when you want to introduce sounds. You can have several at once. You may want them to be heard behind speech so make this clear by writing 'Continues' after you've introduced them. Don't forget to cut them or change them at moments in the script if you want to.

– Plan the scenes and set out the dialogue as for a stage play.
– Write your first draft on alternate lines of your paper so that you have space for revisions.
– Try to create a sense of the difference between your characters by their individual use of language, their accent and their manner of speaking. Show these in your writing of their lines.

Setting out a TV play

– Each scene should have a number, a setting, a note as to whether it is exterior or interior and at what time of day.
– New locations are described briefly, as are new characters.
– Camera instructions can be kept simple. Just specify when you want the camera to show something unusual, otherwise assume it will follow the action. A storyboard can be worked on later to make a 'shooting-script' out of the initial TV script. This is normally done by the director.
– Sound effects need to be included in this initial script. Use SFX in the margin to indicate when you are writing them in the script.

Reading logs

A reading log is a place where you can record your thoughts, questions and impressions while you are reading. It helps you reflect as you read by jotting down notes which you can return to when you are working on coursework assignments. Don't forget to make a note of the page numbers so that you can return to your thoughts later. It is also a place for recording your reflections after group discussion.

You may notice programmes or items on television or articles in newspapers and magazines which are related to these plays in some way. It would be useful to keep some notes or cuttings of anything relevant in your reading log.

The activities which follow are designed to help you build up your reading log. Sometimes you will be asked to prepare for your reading of a play, or to pause for thought, or to predict what the writer might choose to do next. You might also be invited to work with a partner or in a small group to exchange questions and opinions.

Before you start reading

Seagulls

1 In a small group, discuss what you think about public performances of the apparent exercise of mind over matter, for example Uri Geller's seeming ability to bend forks without touching them. Consider the following questions.
    - Is it all trickery?
    - Should people with such powers use them for entertainment?
    - Could these abilities be put to better use?

- Should they have to earn a licence to perform by proving that they are genuine?
- If you discovered that you had such powers, what would you do ?

Not Not Not Not Not Enough Oxygen

1 Watch the news on TV and record how many items of news make you feel sad and how many make you feel happy. Record this for three days and then compare notes with a partner. Discuss the following questions.
   - Is the news mostly distressing?
   - Can the news upset you?
   - Can you eat and watch pictures of starving children or of death and destruction on TV?

2 Record an interview in which you ask a parent if the news is generally worse today than *twenty* years ago. Then record an interview with a grandparent, or a neighbour of similar age, about whether they think the news today is generally worse than it was *forty* years ago. Compare your findings with a partner and make notes on your own conclusions. What do you believe to be the case?

3 In small groups, discuss how you think that in, say, five years' time your opinions might be different from those of one of your parents; for example your views on bringing up children or your political views.
   How do you think your parent might react to discovering this difference of opinion?

The Judge's Wife

1 With a partner discuss which political party you would vote for if you had the vote. Discuss the following questions.

- What is the difference between a socialist and a conservative?
- What is a revolutionary?
- Is it ever right to break the law to try to bring about change or to protest about something?
- Is violent action ever justified in any circumstances to bring about change?
- Are there some people who have an interest in resisting change?
- What changes do you feel are needed in, for example, your community?
- What would be the most appropriate action to bring about changes?

While you are reading

Seagulls

This play was written to be seen on stage so you have to imagine how you would feel in the audience as you read it. The climax on page 14, which keeps the audience waiting for an embarrassingly long time, is specially important. So the best way to experience what Caryl Churchill intended would be to watch a performance of this play. You might like to arrange to do this in your classroom.

1   *Stop reading at page 6 '. . . this is the greatest day of my life.'*
    Discuss with a partner what you think it is that Mrs Valery Blair does.

2   *Stop reading at 'heroes of my childhood' on page 6.*
    Now confirm with your partner that you now know what Valery does.

3   *Stop reading at 'I've talked a lot of nonsense' on page 12.*
    Discuss with a partner whether you agree with Valery's
    statement. What is your impression of her so far?

4   *Stop reading after '. . . feel better if I stopped trying' on page 14.*
    How would you feel at this moment if you were in the
    audience watching this play? If you were Di, what would
    you say to Valery when she comes off-stage? Write this
    dialogue thinking carefully about the way to deal with
    Valery and the kind of person Di has been shown to be so
    far. Now read on to find out how Caryl Churchill has
    decided to develop this.

5   *Read up to when 'Di goes' on page 19.*
    Cliff is about to return to talk to Valery. Write their
    dialogue thinking carefully about Cliff's earlier attitude
    and language. Now read on to see how Caryl Churchill has
    decided to develop this scene.

Not Not Not Not Not Enough Oxygen

This play was originally written to be heard on the radio,
although the text in this book is introduced with details that
would be helpful for a stage performance. In choosing her
title for this radio play, Caryl Churchill has drawn attention to
the speech pattern of one of her characters. Vivian's habit of
repeating herself in a continuous flow of often unfinished
sentences tells the radio listener a lot about her, but makes it
difficult to read her lines at first go. It is best to read them out
aloud if you are reading by yourself. The ideal thing would be
to hear a reading from three people who had prepared and
rehearsed a performance of the play.

1   The play is set in the year 2010, that is forty years in the
    future from the time when it was written. Keep a list of the

details which show how things are different in the world of 2010. Add to this list while you are reading. The first detail is in the words of the play's title.

2   *Stop reading after 'if anyone can afford it Claude Acton' on page 29.*
   With a partner summarise all you know so far about Claude Acton.

3   *Stop reading after 'I haven't come for that' on page 40.*
   What has Claude come for? Discuss this with a partner.

The Judge's Wife

This play was written for television. In order to bring the printed words to life you have to imagine the television production. Think about how the director can tell us the story by shifting the focus from one actor to another and cutting rapidly between sequences (see 'How to read plays', page xviii). You may be able to make a video production of this play to explore its effects upon a TV audience. The play works in a series of steps backwards in time from the opening image.

1   How many steps backwards in time are made in the opening sequence of images in italics on page 45?

2   Discuss with a partner your impressions of the Judge from his opening speech. Which of his statements do you agree with? What do you think of his judgement on Vernon?

3   *Read up to where the Judge goes out on page 57.*
   With a partner list all the key actions and statements of the Judge that have influenced your opinion of him so far.
   Now list the key statements and actions that have influenced your opinion of Caroline.

Not Not Not Not Not Enough Oxygen

and Other Plays

Seagulls

Characters

VALERY, middle-aged

DI, slightly younger

CLIFF, young, American

Green grass, clear sky.

VALERY *and* DI.

DI *looks at her watch.*

VALERY   I don't like it.

DI   What? What don't you like?

VALERY   Can we get tea?

DI   And cakes. I told them you'd like cakes.

VALERY   I don't like the open air.

DI   It's only for charity.

VALERY   I don't eat cakes before.

DI   You do.

VALERY   I don't any more.

DI   You still drink tea?

VALERY   What tea?

DI   You can eat the cakes after.

VALERY   Yes I can, you are lovely Di, I'm sorry I'm so nasty, I'm not in the mood today. I wish we were just here with nothing to do like everyone else. I wish I'd come to see somebody else do something wonderful instead of being the one.

DI   You enjoy it.

VALERY   You don't have to do anything.

DI *looks at her watch.*

DI   We've nothing on the whole of next week except packing and I'll do all that. We can go and watch other people every day. What would you like? We could go to a concert.

VALERY   You know I hate concerts.

3

DI   What then? You don't in fact like watching other people do things.

VALERY   Is there a circus on?

DI   I can find out.

VALERY   I'm like a performing elephant. Di, I really don't enjoy it any more. I'm like a chimpanzee on a bicycle.

DI   If I was a chimpanzee I'd be thankful I could ride a bicycle and not be stuck in a cage all day.

VALERY   I didn't mean you don't have to do anything. You're the one does all the work. I couldn't write letters and talk to people on the phone and make bookings. I wouldn't know how.

DI   But you're the one it's all about. You're the one with the gift.

VALERY   I think I'm a freak.

DI   You know what you are. You're one of the first of a new species of person.

VALERY   Well. It's bound to be tiring.

DI   Of course it is. You're wonderful to keep going the way you do.

VALERY   I expect it's all right in the open air.

DI   Nice to see the sun for once.

VALERY   It smells nice. I never like the smell in laboratories. I don't expect I'll ever see daylight once I'm at Harvard.

DI   And don't pretend you won't love it.

VALERY   There's quite a lot of people.

DI   Naturally.

VALERY   And I'll just do it, and they'll all clap, and then it's done and we'll have tea and cakes. I'll have made all that money for – what?

DI   There's a young man waiting. I said you probably wouldn't see him.

VALERY   What sort of young man?

DI   Nothing special.

VALERY   No.

DI   What I'm really looking forward to after you're finished with your scientists is the whole US tour. It's a dream to me. Chicago. Los Angeles. Little Rock Arkansas. New place every day. People cheering. You don't know who you'll meet. And next morning you just leave again.

VALERY   Will people cheer?

DI   Of course.

VALERY   I suppose they will.

DI   You wouldn't rather be working in Marks and Spencer's?

VALERY   I might see that young man if you could find the tea.

DI *looks at her watch.*

DI   Don't put yourself out.

DI *goes.*

CLIFF *enters.*

CLIFF   Mrs Blair? It's very kind of you.

VALERY   Not at all.

CLIFF   I know how sick you must get of fans.

VALERY   Not really.

5

CLIFF And just before appearing too. I thought you would probably have to rest.

VALERY No, I just have a cup of tea.

CLIFF I would have thought you'd have to prepare yourself. Like sit in solitude for a period of time and summon all your innermost energies.

VALERY Not all that much, no.

CLIFF You just go out there and do it? Mrs Blair, I have to say this, this is the greatest day of my life. That may sound foolish to you –

VALERY No.

CLIFF I've followed your career ever since I was a child. Before you got famous this last year or so I knew about you already because there was a newspaper story back in seventy-two about that time you were mad at your husband and objects such as frying pans and dishes started to fly through the air without you touching them. And you denied it, you know, but I thought this has got to be true. I pinned the cutting up by my bed. I was thirteen at the time and my dad was kind of a heavy drinker, well he still is, and I'll tell you, you and Flash Gordon were the two heroes of my childhood.

VALERY I don't know Flash Gordon.

CLIFF Mrs Blair, may I ask you something?

VALERY Please do.

CLIFF Why did you deny it? Why did you keep the world waiting five years?

VALERY I don't know really.

CLIFF My friends used to laugh at me.

VALERY I wasn't ready. I didn't mean it to happen.

CLIFF   You didn't? You mean it just happened? I've wondered about that. What did you think just before it started happening?

VALERY   You see, I don't remember.

CLIFF   What was the last thing you said? Were you just so mad at him or what?

VALERY   I don't remember.

CLIFF   What had he done just before that to make you – I'm sorry. I do apologise. I have thought about this a great deal.

VALERY   My little girls were only five and seven years old.

CLIFF   I beg your pardon?

VALERY   That's why I said I threw the frying pan with my hands. I didn't want to start – well, all this, I didn't know what it would start if I said I could move things.

CLIFF   You denied it for the sake of your children?

VALERY   I thought it would be more like other children for them if I said I'd just thrown the frying pan.

CLIFF   That's terrible. Children don't like their mothers repressing themselves.

VALERY   They were upset enough as it was.

CLIFF   I have been a child myself quite recently.

VALERY   But it wasn't that important to me. It was only that it got in the papers. I'd always moved things. When I was a child I thought everyone could do it.

CLIFF   Did you really? I think that's beautiful.

VALERY   Well it was stupid, wasn't it? I must have been very unobservant.

CLIFF   And when did it dawn on you you were specially chosen?

7

VALERY   I sort of forgot about it because it obviously wasn't something important like learning to read that your parents cared how you were getting on with it. I felt maybe it was like picking your nose or farting, everyone did it and pretended it didn't happen. So most of the time I forgot about it.

CLIFF   Until one day – ?

VALERY   No, it was just off and on, and in between I wouldn't think about it. I knew it wasn't normal.

CLIFF   You must have felt very proud.

VALERY   No, I didn't then.

CLIFF   You could hardly avoid it now.

VALERY   Well I do feel proud sometimes, I must admit. But then I get tired of it you know, I get bored with it.

CLIFF   You must get very upset when some people think it's all a fake.

VALERY   I'd think it was all a fake if someone else did it.

CLIFF   I think that's wonderful of you.

VALERY   I'm a very ordinary person.

CLIFF   No, Mrs Blair.

VALERY   Well I'm going to Harvard University in America next week for intensive investigations.

CLIFF   You know the US trains dolphins as a weapon of war. You want to be very careful.

VALERY   I only move quite small things quite small distances.

CLIFF   But potentially. You must feel that yourself.

VALERY   Well I do. I must admit.

CLIFF It's the next thing after nuclear physics. Mind is the energy resource of the future.

VALERY It's a funny feeling being so important.

CLIFF Don't let them flatter you. It's how you use it.

VALERY I don't usually like to say because it sounds silly or greedy but it does seem to me sometimes that the mind could really move mountains. I'm not saying my mind you understand, many many minds, if there were many minds that could do it, and maybe in the future, if it's true that I'm ahead of my time, if this is the way people are going to turn out or if everyone really can do it already –

CLIFF Like you thought as a child.

VALERY If they can and just haven't quite got the knack yet, then all those minds together could I don't know what. Send a rocket into space at least, I should think.

DI *comes in with a tray of tea which she puts on the ground.*
VALERY *ignores her and the tea.*
DI *looks at her watch.*

DI Don't exhaust yourself, dear, will you.

DI *goes.*

CLIFF Was that a hint I should leave now?

VALERY Is that silly, do you think, a rocket into space?

CLIFF No, it's absolutely probable.

VALERY This afternoon I have to set off a firework. I just have to move a little knob and that sets off I don't know what but anyway it lights the fuse and off goes a rocket.

CLIFF I think that's a really great symbol of what lies ahead.

VALERY I do too. I sometimes think can this be me? I was working in Marks and Spencer's, you may know that –

CLIFF   I do indeed, and how you caught the shoplifter. That's legendary, Mrs Blair.

VALERY   I think deep down I must have decided it was time I did something.

CLIFF   You had this secret power.

VALERY   Everybody thought I was just an ordinary person and I'm not clever or pretty. If I had to say all I know about inflation or protecting the whale I'd be finished in thirty seconds. I've no skills, well I can run a home but you don't feel that's enough these days, my mother could just stay home and not worry but then she wasn't happy either. So there I was at Marks and the novelty of that had worn off, because at first it was a novelty just to go out to work again, I thought I can't go to work looking like this, I felt shy. But of course you get used to it very quickly, I wished it had been harder because I was already bored and bored at home too because it's very up and down and the girls are getting on. Some days it seemed nobody had spoken to me all day, well nobody had looked me in the eye, just nothing at all had happened. Things had happened of course but not so the end of the day would be any different from the beginning, and I'd had enough because of course I knew what I could do. I think I chose catching the shoplifter to get a big fuss, because I said to Di, that's Di that's my manager now, she was working there, that's how I knew her, I said Di, look, and I didn't do it till she was looking. Then I made the shirt he'd taken come right back up out of the bag and on to the counter. And that was it really and it's been non-stop from that moment and my whole way of life, you can imagine. But my daughters quite like it because everyone at school says they've seen me on television, and I'm not away all that much. And I think my husband thinks more of me than when I was nobody. And I do like it. I like it when what I'm looking at starts to move, and then everyone's amazed, and the professors talk to you like someone who understands, and you get to meet people and go places you never would, and it's only sometimes lately like today I haven't felt like doing it, and even sometimes I find I can't do it. At home sometimes I think shall I try, shall I do it, and it's like when you can't remember a word or you can't swallow, have you ever had that, sometimes for a split second you can't swallow, my God, and then it's all right, sometimes it's like that, I can't do it, I think my God. And then either it's all right again or else I just don't do it, I leave it, I do it some other time, I leave it because it's no use panicking. And I seem to get more tired now. When I was a child I'd never feel any effect from it but after a day in a science laboratory, well it's harder work, my pulse rate goes up to four times normal and my brain waves do extraordinary things if you see afterwards where they've recorded it, and I'm just exhausted for hours sometimes, I lie there and I can't wake up or go to sleep and I think one day I'm going to die of this. But then next day I'm back again because I suppose it has a fascination for me so I keep trying, but when I was young I used to do it so easily or even without knowing like the time you read about when the frying pans and dishes flew across the room and one of them did in fact catch my husband on the ear, but of course I pretended I threw them and everyone thought he was crazy or drunk, which he was anyway, but now of course all his friends –

She stops.

CLIFF   What?

VALERY   What?

CLIFF   You were saying?

VALERY   What?

11

CLIFF   You were saying your husband's friends . . .? Now appreciate how right he was and realise the truth of what an amazing woman you are.

VALERY   Please go away.

CLIFF   Mrs Blair?

VALERY   I've talked a lot of nonsense.

CLIFF   Believe me –

VALERY   I'm tired.

CLIFF   Yes of course, I'm sorry, you must rest and get yourself together for the great moment. I can't tell you how grateful I am for the opportunity –

VALERY   Di! Di!

CLIFF   Shall I find her for you?

DI *enters.*

VALERY   Di, I don't feel well.

DI   What have you been saying to her?

CLIFF   She's the one who's been doing the talking.

DI   Off you go now, leave her alone.

CLIFF   Goodbye, Mrs Blair. I hope you feel better. And believe me it's been a great honour. God, I never got her autograph. Do you think – no, sorry. Goodbye. Sorry.

CLIFF *goes.*

DI *looks at her watch.*

VALERY   Di?

DI   There now.

VALERY   What the hell did you let me see him for?

12

DI   You said you wanted to.

VALERY   I hate talking.

DI   I thought a fan would give you a bit of a lift.

VALERY   It did at first but now I feel terrible.

DI   You haven't drunk your tea.

VALERY   I talked too much.

DI   Just be quiet for a bit.

VALERY   I talked such a lot of nonsense.

DI   Here, drink this.

VALERY   Mind you, he talked a lot of nonsense.

DI   I'm sure he did. You shouldn't give your time to these people.

VALERY   They don't understand and they will keep talking about it till it gets to be something quite different. I'm not seeing anybody afterwards. I'm never seeing anyone again.

DI   You don't have to.

VALERY   I hate talking about it, Di. I shouldn't talk about it. I should just do it. I don't like talking.

DI   In ten minutes you are going to do it.

VALERY   The tea's cold.

DI   It would be by now.

VALERY   It doesn't matter.

DI   Hush now.

VALERY   Di.

DI   Yes, love.

VALERY   It doesn't really matter.

DI   What doesn't?

VALERY   Talking.

DI   Of course not, you deserve a bit of fun. Just you mustn't get tired out, that's all.

VALERY   It doesn't matter because I'm going to do it in a minute, and that's all that matters, nothing else really. Hardly anything. Really nothing else matters to me Di except this.

DI *looks at her watch.*
The light brightens.
The machine is an elaborate mechanism inside a glass dome with a rocket attached at one side.

VALERY *stands by it, not moving.*

DI *is standing well back and to one side.*

VALERY *smiles. Then she is grave. She concentrates.*
This goes on.
Her face is red with effort.
She half looks round at DI, DI *half steps forward, but* VALERY *turns back.* DI *stays where she is.*
She goes on and on, motionless.

VALERY   I think we'd all feel better if I stopped trying.

DI *and* VALERY. VALERY *is sitting on the ground. She puts aside a half-eaten cake.*

DI   My aunt's a remarkable woman. When her husband died she cried for a week and then for another week she didn't say a word, just sat staring at the wall. At the end of that time she went out and bought a wig and joined an amateur dramatic society. She was eighty-two. She went on holiday last summer to Italy. She said, 'The only thing I didn't like dear was all those old women sitting outside their houses dressed in black.' Don't you think we might go on holiday?

VALERY   I don't know.

DI   We could go for a week in Majorca.

VALERY   I want to go home.

DI   I'm seriously considering postponing Harvard.

VALERY   How can we?

DI   We can do what we like.

VALERY   They're busy men. They've got other work to do.

DI   They're not unique, Valery. You are.

VALERY   I don't want to go to Harvard.

DI   Two weeks in Majorca.

VALERY   I'd miss the children too much.

DI   We'll take the children. You can have two weeks in Majorca with your husband and children without me, if that's what you want.

VALERY   He couldn't take a holiday this time of year.

DI   You and the children then. You and me and the children.

VALERY   Do be quiet.

DI   You're just exhausted, that's all.

VALERY   All the people. Were they given their money back?

DI   If they ask for it. But they're not asking because it was for charity. And anyway they did see you, you did try, it's not as if they didn't see anything. People enjoy watching things go wrong.

VALERY   We can't afford a holiday, Di, because I won't be earning any more.

DI   Of course you will.

VALERY   No, I'm finished.

DI   You just need a rest.

VALERY   No.

DI   You'll have a complete medical tomorrow.

VALERY   I'm not ill. I'm perfectly normal. I just can't do it any more.

DI   Of course you can.

VALERY   No I can't.

DI   All right, you're finished, it's over.

VALERY   Do you think so?

DI   I don't know, do I? It could be.

VALERY   I'm just tired.

DI   Maybe.

VALERY   I shouldn't have talked so much.

DI   You think it was that?

VALERY   I've stayed up all night and still moved things. I lifted a table three feet into the air when I was drunk without spilling a glass.

DI   Look Valery, don't start feeling sorry for yourself. If you think you're tired, then take a rest. Do whatever you need to get it working again and never mind the expense, it's an investment. This is our whole living at stake.

VALERY   All right then. We'll take a holiday. Then we'll go to Harvard.

DI   Postpone Harvard?

VALERY   A week?

DI   Two weeks.

VALERY   What about the tour? What about all the bookings?

DI   Look I'm the manager, will you leave me to manage? I'm not panicking. I'm not saying it can't be done. Just get well as fast as you f★★★★★★ can.

VALERY   I'm not ill.

DI   Get working.

VALERY   I'm going to, my God, I miss once and you start acting like this. You'd still be in the shirt department if I hadn't let you be my manager. You can't move objects with your mind. You don't understand anything at all about it. You're nothing. I can always get another manager.

DI   If you can still do it, Valery, you can have ten managers tomorrow. On the other hand if you can't do it, there's nothing to manage, you're the one who's nothing. I've had considerable experience this year, I've got considerable contacts, I can always get other clients. I can start an agency.

VALERY   Of course I can still do it. It's just because it was in the open air. I can't concentrate in the sunshine.

DI   I always knew you wouldn't last but I thought you'd last longer than this.

VALERY   You're fired.

DI   You're not a job any more, there's nothing to be fired from. You never really wanted to succeed. You're frightened of it. You'd rather be sorry for yourself, it's what you're used to. You don't want to go to America, you're not up to it, you're just little Mrs Blair that's all, you want to go home to your family and make the tea, and a few half-days in Marks and Spencer's. But I'm a businesswoman. I'm on my way.

And if you're not going up any more I'll find someone who is, because there's plenty of them.

VALERY   It wasn't about that. It was something I could do in my mind and now I can't. Unless I still can. I'll wait and see. I'll find out in the end.

DI   Valery. Why don't you just nudge that teacup and see if it goes?

VALERY   No.

DI   Go on.

VALERY   I don't want to.

DI   If you can't it wouldn't make things any worse. And if you can, then –

VALERY   I don't want to try.

DI   I'm sorry for what I said.

VALERY   Never mind. I expect I started it.

DI   I won't really leave you.

VALERY   I don't want you to.

DI   That's all right then.

VALERY   Well it's not, is it?

DI   Everyone's entitled to an off day.

VALERY   It's not the first time. It's been getting worse.

DI   It is the first time.

VALERY   It's the first time in public.

DI   You might have said. If I make bookings I'm saying this is something good. I'm going to look foolish.

VALERY   So that's why I'm frightened.

DI   I won't leave you.

VALERY   Not yet you won't, just in case. But you will after.

DI   You know something we could do. If you could just make it through Harvard so you've got your scientific guarantee, and then for the tour maybe we could find some way of working it.

VALERY   Working it?

DI   Fixing it. No, well, I didn't think you'd leap at that. Shall we go home?

VALERY   Go away, will you?

DI   I'll be in the car.

VALERY   I'm getting a train.

DI   Don't sulk, Valery.

VALERY   I'll see you tomorrow.

DI   Have you got enough money on you?

DI *goes.*

CLIFF *enters.*

CLIFF   My first reaction was just to slink off. And then I thought, well everybody's just going to have slunk off and maybe you'd feel better if someone – anyway you only have to say and I'll . . .

VALERY   It's very nice of you to bother.

CLIFF   It's a kind of hard situation to know what to say in.

VALERY   I'm sorry I let you down.

CLIFF   No no, I'm sorry, I mean you must feel terrible. I know I feel terrible. But I've been thinking and you know what it is, it's just embarrassment. It was just appallingly embarrassing. Like when I was six I went to the bathroom in my pants in the museum and everyone was saying, What's this awful smell? So I joined in, I said, What's this awful smell? And then some of this shit ran down my leg and made this trail behind me on the floor of the museum, and one of the kids saw it and they all said, What's that? And I joined in, I said, What's that guck on the floor? And they all knew it was me, and I knew they knew it was me, and I still said, What's that on the floor? That was my previous most embarrassing moment. But embarrassment's nothing really. You'll go on and do it fine and land rockets on the moon and your name will go down in all history books and statues to you in public places with pigeons on and people calling their babies Valery.

VALERY   If I can't do it any more, I won't have this tour in America or anything. I won't have people coming round after to see me.

CLIFF   You're still the person who did it before. You're still Flash Gordon.

VALERY   Not if I can't do it.

CLIFF   But if you did it before, even if you'd only done it once, there's bound to be other people. It's not a matter of you, it's a matter of human potential. I guess you're not too interested in human potential this afternoon.

VALERY   I don't know if you still want my autograph.

CLIFF   Of course, yes please. Really , I was going to ask you.

VALERY   Best wishes to – ?

CLIFF   Cliff.

VALERY   Cliff. There. Thank you.

CLIFF   Thank you. Look there's a story I thought about while I was watching you struggling away. I don't know if you can stand Chinese wisdom. There was this man and all the seagulls came down round him and lit on his head and his hands every time he went down on the beach. And one day his father was very sick, and he said to his son, Go down on the beach and get me a seagull, I'm lying here in bed and I'd really like to see a seagull. So his son goes down on the beach and not one seagull comes near him. I wonder if that's relevant at all.

VALERY   I don't see what it has to do with the Chinese.

CLIFF   I mean whether it's doing it for money, or doing it when you're bored with it, or doing it in laboratories, or doing it when you want to too much, or whether it's just packed up like somebody going blind. The fact that you can't do it is in a way just as interesting as the fact that you could do it. Somebody could do a whole study about what causes these things not to happen.

VALERY   We don't know for certain I can't do it.

CLIFF   Of course we don't.

VALERY   You're talking about me as if I'm dead.

CLIFF   I'm sorry.

VALERY   You can't do it and you're still alive. Everybody I see is walking around and they can't move heavy objects with the power of their minds, and they don't want to kill themselves because of that. What keeps them going?

CLIFF   Different things. I guess you've got used to being extra-ordinary.

VALERY   I sit here looking and there's the people and the trees and the grass, and things are still moving. Or not moving. It's just that I can't . . .

CLIFF   There's plenty going on all right.

21

VALERY   You can't do it either.

CLIFF   I'll do something else. I haven't even finished college yet. If you do get to the States I'll certainly come to one of your showings. You know I bet some people won't believe you couldn't do it today. They'll think you pretended to get everyone more interested. And people who think it's all a fake anyway will think you pretended to make it seem more real. I don't really like to say this, but until today I kind of always wondered if it was a fake. In fact, even when I saw you couldn't do it, it just lurked in the corner of my mind that it might be a really great con trick. Even now I wouldn't bet my life on it. I nearly would.

VALERY   I loved it. It was all that mattered.

CLIFF   That was another embarrassing moment.

VALERY   It's rather cold.

CLIFF   I love your English summers. I think they're neat. You get these really unexpected skies. What are you doing?

VALERY   Nothing.

CLIFF   I thought for a minute maybe . . . you know . . . moving the teacup or something. No. Sorry.

VALERY   No. No, I'm just watching.

CLIFF   Watching what?

VALERY   Watching things move.

Not Not Not Not Not Enough Oxygen

Characters

VIVIAN

MICK

CLAUDE

VIVIAN is 30. She dresses to look young but her face looks older, very pale and ill.
MICK is 60. He has dressed carefully in his best clothes.
CLAUDE is 19. He has very fair hair, cut short, and is beautiful. His clothes are expensive but crumpled and dusty.

The time is 2010. Mick was young in the seventies. Clothes shouldn't look space-age but different from contemporary ones. Mick perhaps likes the bright colours of his youth, now old-fashioned. Claude might wear a dark suit.

The place is Mick's one room in a tower block. It is small, brightly painted and very cluttered: bed, table, chairs, etc., including one large old-fashioned armchair; TV; music; books; games; puzzles; large jigsaw half-finished on a table; jug of water and glasses; intercom by the door for speaking to the front door downstairs; one window, shut, looking out to smoggy sky.

Not Not Not Not Not Enough Oxygen was first broadcast on BBC Radio 3, 31 March 1971. The cast was as follows:

VIVIAN   *Barbara Mitchell*
MICK   *John Hollis*
CLAUDE   *Clive Merrison*

Produced by John Tydeman

VIVIAN Shall I tell you what what I bought today? Not enough enough oxygen in this block, why always headache. Spoke caretaker, caretaker says speak manager, manager says local authority local authority won't give us won't give us the money. Said I said what's the no point giving us faster – all be dead corpses in the faster lifts if there's not not not not not enough oxygen. Caretaker caretaker said his part his personal if it was up to if it was down to him would put big plants big plants plants plants in every room. Do stop walking about, Mick. Mick, do keep still as if you were paying as if you were hearing me.

MICK I'm waiting for my son.

VIVIAN Listen, it will take your mind take your mind off. What I said plants plants would take money. Earth plants earth would all have to come in from the park and the park the park authority the park authority wouldn't permit. Because hardly any park hardly any park left. My sister told me she went went went went to, four days four days days days to get and the crowd was the crowd was the crowd was just like home.

MICK How late will he be?

VIVIAN The grass can only – Mick why not go up on the roof and walk about walk about about in the haze? There's no room in this room in this room. You take five five steps remind that mad cat cat in cage at the zoo up and up and down up and –

He sits down.

Yes sit do sit and breathe quietly. Breathe quietly. It was Claude's own it was Claude said his own idea to come so he will. Shall we do some more of the big jig big jigsaw?

MICK *pays no attention.*

The grass. The grass in the park the grass can only be seen over the over the over the heads heads of the crowd and fenced off so you can see see some because of course where the crowd walks where the crowd walks it's just mud. So what I bought what I bought was look an oxygen spray and spray spray oxygen in the room. (*She sprays it.*)

MICK   Yes, spray it about. Let's have plenty of it. Don't spare. Claude will see his poor old dad knows how to live. He can give me all the money he likes and be sure I'll make good use of it. Not like his mother, who won't take a pound from him. Say nothing about her. But I know what money buys. I can enjoy a fortune.

VIVIAN   I can I can too.

MICK   Your husband earns.

VIVIAN   Mick you know I only only I only live with him for the room. Where where else can I go where can I go if you won't won't have me in your room to live?

MICK   It's too small for two.

VIVIAN   All the rooms are the same are the same size.

MICK   All too small.

VIVIAN   But you know I feel nothing nothing I feel nothing for him only you.

MICK   An old man.

VIVIAN   Not not an old man.

MICK   An old man.

VIVIAN   Not very very.

MICK   Not at all. Not old at all. When I was young there were men my age who did a day's work. I could work. My body is a bit out of use. But I can still touch my toes. My mind is a bit – my mind is not stretched. We must get some new puzzles. I am at an age where the things that go wrong with me won't get right again. But not much wrong. Claude will see quite a fine old man.

VIVIAN   He'll be proud proud of his father.

MICK   Proud? Do you think?

VIVIAN   'I hope I'm as handsome handsome as you Dad when I'm as old as your age,' Claude Claude will say.

MICK   He gets his looks from me. His mother had a certain brightness but not so much the shape of feature. You weren't born when I was his age so you missed all that happy time. I had fair hair, long fair hair, long was the thing then. But Claude's better looking than I was. The last time I saw him he sat in this chair. His mother stood there by the window. She'd brought him to say goodbye. He'd won a scholarship to his college in Africa. He was fourteen. His face – oh a brilliant child.

VIVIAN   Did he look look like he looks when you see him see him sing?

MICK   Sometimes when I see him in a programme – you'll laugh.

VIVIAN   I never never laugh.

MICK   If I'm alone sometimes I kiss him. That is to say I kneel down and put my mouth to the screen. Father and son counts even today. Then of course I find the picture has changed. I'm kissing an announcer or a tank. I feel a fool. But thousands of little girls must do the same.

VIVIAN   When he comes shall I go shall I go out?

MICK   Out? Out in the street?

VIVIAN   Of course not out in the street in the street do you

27

think I'm mad? Out of the room out out of the way, down in the down down in the lift to my room or the shops.

MICK Don't you want to meet him?

VIVIAN But it's five years since you haven't seen him for five years.

MICK He'll give you his autograph if I ask him.

VIVIAN You'll want to want to talk talk heart to not with a stranger not with me here.

MICK No. No no. You must stay. I haven't seen him for five years. You're still young. You can help us speak to each other.

VIVIAN I should like to be able to say I'd seen seen him spoken spoken to Claude Acton spoken to Claude Acton perhaps touched him.

MICK He'll like you. Who knows? There may be money for you. He's a sweet good kind boy. He has given money to strangers.

VIVIAN To me to me me do you think?

MICK If not never mind. He'll give me so much I can give you what you like. A daily dress. Eggs. Oxygen.

VIVIAN Mick, if you do do do get a cottage in the cottage in cottage in the park –

MICK Yes, I'm going to get a cottage.

VIVIAN Mick, I shall stay I shall stay with you because I want to get out get out of the Londons and not live in a tower tower tower block and you would have enough room you would you would have enough room for me there. And though you're in middle late late middle age I shall I shall I shall stay with you though I'm still young and look

28

look younger than I am if you want if if if you want me if you want me.

MICK   Yes, I'd like that. It's something isn't it to be happy at times and make someone happy. Let's stay together a long time shall we, because I like you.

VIVIAN   I wish wish we could go go away now. I wish he would hurry hurry and get here. I'll look out and see if there's a car in the car in the jam. He must have a car a car licence to bring a car in the Londons if anyone can afford it Claude Acton.

MICK   You look. I'm too shortsighted. I can't make out the street.

VIVIAN *peers down at the street without opening the window.*

VIVIAN   Not not your eyes it's the fumes and fumes and haze. I can hardly hardly – no no only buses buses only buses hardly moving today. There's a fire.

MICK   Near?

VIVIAN   No, do you see do you see black smoke far over far over there?

MICK   Those fanatics said they'd do something or other today. Did you see on the news?

VIVIAN   No, but what what kill themselves I suppose.

MICK   Themselves or others.

VIVIAN   At night night in the night I'm afraid I'm afraid Mick I'm afraid if I wake in the night I think the block the block is going to go up to go up in flames any any any any moment go up in – ah!

MICK   What? Is it him?

VIVIAN   Look look.

29

MICK   Where?

VIVIAN   I think I think it was a bird it was a bird a bird bird a bird.

MICK   What? What?

VIVIAN   Bird.

MICK   A bird in the Londons?

VIVIAN   Small brown brown I think it was a bird.

MICK   A sparrow. A sparrow is a small brown bird. I didn't see it.

VIVIAN   Shall I open open open the window?

MICK   No.

VIVIAN   Yes yes yes you might see.

She opens the window. The distant roar of traffic.

MICK   Shut it at once. The haze. The stink. Uh.

VIVIAN *shuts the window.*

Spray your oxygen about. You'll kill me.

VIVIAN   (*spraying oxygen*) But the bird was a good a good-luck sign good luck for us, Mick.

MICK   Claude can't have seen a sparrow. He's not twenty.

VIVIAN   I remember I remember birds but bigger than that, it shows I'm not so young not so young as I – well I am thirty thirty had you thought? But what's youth youth youth these days? They don't enjoy enjoy any more and I can still I can still enjoy enjoy myself and you can you can.

MICK   There were still some birds in the eighties. When I was a young man there were flocks of birds. What you remember is pigeons. Now they were a plague before elimination. They fouled the towers. I have honked the horn of my car in London streets at flocks of pigeons pecking at the bread thrown to them by some old woman dead now. And birds whose names you may have seen at the zoo, blackbird, starling, bluetit, I have seen them with my own eyes wild in the gardens of the Londons long ago.

The doorbell rings.

VIVIAN Mick Mick.

MICK He's come.

VIVIAN Mick press the press press the buzzer buzzer press the buzzer.

MICK (*into intercom*) Who is it? Claude?

A buzzy voice replies.

(MICK *presses the buzzer to open the downstairs door.*) Come up, come up.

VIVIAN Now at last the new fast some point at last in the new fast fast lift. He'll be here here at any in a moment at any moment he'll be he'll be here oh Mick he'll –

The doorbell rings.

MICK Open the door, Vivian.

VIVIAN Do I look look do I look all all right?

MICK Open the door.

VIVIAN (*opening the door*) Come in come come in.

CLAUDE *comes in unsteadily and stops.*

MICK Claude, my Claude, Claude. How tall you are. You haven't changed. Is it really you? (*He comes towards* CLAUDE.)

VIVIAN We've been waiting waiting –

MICK   Do you feel all right? You look pale.

CLAUDE *collapses.*

VIVIAN   Careful.

MICK   He's falling.

VIVIAN   Fainting he's fainting.

MICK   Chair.

VIVIAN   Here in the chair chair here here in the chair in the chair.

They sit him in a chair. Pause.

CLAUDE   Be all right. Wait.

MICK   Get some water.

VIVIAN *gets some.*

CLAUDE   Just sit a minute.

MICK   Claude, are you ill? What's happened? How can I get a doctor?

VIVIAN   Here here you are, water here's some water.

MICK   Have a sip of water, Claude. I've got the glass. There. There.

CLAUDE   All right. Thank you. Better.

VIVIAN   What what shall I do?

CLAUDE   Nothing. All right. Thank you. Sorry. Didn't know how far how far it would be.

MICK   How far?

VIVIAN   In the traffic the traffic the jam.

MICK   You're tired out by sitting so long in the car.

CLAUDE   Walked.

VIVIAN   Walked walked Mick he walked.

VIVIAN   Walked, Claude? Where from? Did the car break down?

VIVIAN   Programme I saw programme said might be quicker to walk walk in the Londons than buses if only the air –

MICK   Where is the car? Is it safe?

CLAUDE   No car.

MICK   But you have, Claude.

CLAUDE   Did have.

MICK   Was it stolen?

VIVIAN   The crime rate the crime –

CLAUDE   No no, got rid of it, I – got rid of it. Thought I'd like to walk. Do like. Just far.

MICK   But to walk in the Londons. The air. The danger. You'll meet fanatics out in the open like that. They kill you. You must never do it again. What if you'd fainted in the street?

CLAUDE   I'm here.

VIVIAN   But someone famous famous like you to walk –

CLAUDE   Please don't.

VIVIAN   – walk in the Londons only fanatics and bad bad –

CLAUDE   Please.

MICK   Well it's lovely to see you, Claude.

VIVIAN   Let me spray some oxygen oxygen spray. Do you good and I feel I feel I need something I need something. (*She sprays oxygen.*)

CLAUDE   Wanted to see you. You're all right?

MICK   Oh yes. Yes. I make the best of what I can get. The little room is hard to bear because of course I remember the old days when people had more than one room. I don't get out of course. But I change the colour scheme from time to time. It's not a bad block. Large television. Lots of music. We complain about the air but the plumbing works. We've no sewage problem. There's no water of course but that's the same anywhere. I have books. I read. It passes time. And puzzles. All kinds of puzzle. Jigsaw, Chinese, mind tickles in the paper. Vivian and I do puzzles sometimes all day. We follow your movements when we can. You've been in China just now. It makes us feel less shut in.

CLAUDE   You hear from mother?

MICK   Hear from your mother? Now and then.

CLAUDE   She's gone off, hasn't she? Gave up all her gave up all her things. Not that she had much, she was never – Tried to give her – when I first earned – but she wouldn't. February she wrote me she'd formally relinquished her room, burnt her cards, just gone. So many do.

VIVIAN   Not many in the normal normal way only fanatics –

CLAUDE   That's what she is of course if you call them that.

MICK   I never did understand your mother. She was always sad about one thing or another. I used to turn the news off, it upset her so much. Twenty years ago. The news is very much worse now and it must have turned her mind, poor woman.

VIVIAN   It's a madness they say sweeping the country sweeping all the countries they say.

CLAUDE   What about Alexander?

MICK   Alexander? No, I'm out of touch.

VIVIAN   Who? Alexander who? I don't know who Alexander –

CLAUDE   My half-brother.

MICK   Yes I have an older son, much older. By my first marriage, which I have just mentioned, I think. My first wife married again. She did well. A rich man. She flies. You may meet as you go about, do you Claude?

CLAUDE   Once or twice.

MICK   Tell me about her.

CLAUDE   Very striking still from a distance. Armed guard always of course because stones are thrown. But laughing it off.

MICK   Alexander doesn't keep in touch. He was always too full of ideals. His wife is a doctor too?

CLAUDE   Do you not know then about the baby?

MICK   They had a baby? Did they?

CLAUDE   Wife wouldn't have another abortion though hadn't got exemption. They kept moving country to country to avoid the regulations. Born in Egypt I think.

MICK   Boy or girl?

CLAUDE   It died.

VIVIAN   Oh no how sad how sad why did it die?

CLAUDE   They killed it.

VIVIAN   Why why why did they why?

CLAUDE   They changed their minds. It cleared their conscience. It wasn't a licensed child.

MICK   I would rather not have known about it, Claude.

CLAUDE   I'd rather you did know about it.

35

VIVIAN   Were they sent sent to prison were they sentenced to prison?

CLAUDE   Five years for evading abortion but suspended since the child was dead. Gone as doctors to one of the epidemic areas now so no more to hear of them.

MICK   Alexander was a pretty baby.

VIVIAN   Babies are always always pretty and make you want want one if you see if you see a baby I want one but they shouldn't evade I've never dared never dared evade the regulations. But if I did if I did have if I did have one have a baby I couldn't I couldn't kill it more than kill myself I couldn't kill –

MICK   With all his mother's money Alexander could have bought a licence.

CLAUDE   Went in for the lottery. Thinks it's wrong to buy licences. So do I.

MICK   You mean you'll go in for the lottery? With your money? What do you earn it for if you won't use it?

CLAUDE   Won't have a child at all.

MICK   You're young yet. Don't let's quarrel about it.

VIVIAN   It's fanatic to kill a fanatic to kill a baby like killing yourself killing myself I'd never but fanatics do do do it hundred at a time I saw saw last night on the news a hundred hundred in a burning block some singing singing and some screaming and today today they say there are more more something going to happen. Life in the life in the Londons is no fun no no fun these days and the sooner we go to the park go to the park –

CLAUDE   Going to the park?

MICK   It's what I hope for.

CLAUDE   Live there?

MICK   It's all I want.

CLAUDE   Got money then?

MICK   Not yet.

CLAUDE   Be better off with my mother walking about. Still open country some places. Risk is you starve of course like most people. I've seen that. Given what I can but five million pounds goes in a day.

VIVIAN   You've given given five million five five million pounds?

CLAUDE   Yes.

VIVIAN   You're even richer than I thought richer than how many millions many millions have you got left?

CLAUDE   None.

MICK   Not so much as a million?

CLAUDE   Gave it away.

VIVIAN   All all gave it all?

CLAUDE   Yes.

MICK   All to strangers?

VIVIAN   But we watch we watch the news all the time to see you and it never –

CLAUDE   Did it this morning. Got rid of all my things and sent the telegram I was coming to see you.

VIVIAN   No oh no Mick Mick I'm frightened.

MICK   What about me, Claude?

CLAUDE   Wanted to see you.

MICK   You could have spared me half a million. A couple of hundred thousand. For your father.

CLAUDE   You wanted money?

MICK   My cottage.

CLAUDE   Didn't think of you. You're alive here.

MICK   You didn't think? You didn't think of me? Of course you did. Your father sitting here in his little box? I think of you all the time. You were one of the last children born in the Londons. People used to crowd round your pram because you were beautiful even then. What do you think a licence cost to have a second child? Can't you even pay that money back? How dare you give five million pounds away to strangers?

CLAUDE   People do.

MICK   Oh I know that, it's the fashion isn't it? When I was young we had more sense.

VIVIAN   Mick don't Mick don't make him angry.

MICK   Do you think no one was starving then? In the sixties, seventies, eighties? Do you think there weren't any wars when I was a young man? You're not the first person to see horrors. We learnt to watch them without feeling a thing. We could see pictures of starving children and still eat our dinner while we watched. That's what we need to survive. Your mother was no good at it so her mind went and she's gone off to die in a jungle gnawing a leaf or some nonsense. There's still meat in the Londons if you can pay. There's rations of food and water for each room. We can stay alive if we stay in the blocks. I told her that but she would go. She came to see me. She came at night. I was frightened when I heard the bell but I let her in. Do you know what she said? 'Come and let us end our lives together.' I was always fond of her. I said she could move back in here with me but she wouldn't do it. She would be off. She looked older than me. She said, 'Let me listen to some music and have a really good drink of water because I won't be able just to turn on music and water any more.' I turned on some music and gave her water with ice in it. 'I could almost stay,' she said. Then she got up and out she went without a word.

CLAUDE   You should have gone.

VIVIAN   Mick don't you see what he see what he is?

MICK   I'm not saying I like it here. The rich get out. You could have got me out.

CLAUDE   Half a million to put you in the park? You'd be better dead.

MICK   What do you know about dying?

VIVIAN   Mick stop stop Mick.

MICK   I could talk about dying when I was young. Let go of me, Vivian. Now I'm going to die soon enough. I only need a little pleasure.

VIVIAN   Mick don't you see see how he looks how he looks at you? Don't you see why why he's come he's a fanatic Mick come to kill us kill kill kill us come to kill us.

MICK   Is she right?

VIVIAN   I knew knew always knew fanatic fanatic would come and kill, always saying millions dying hunger dying war hunger war every day so we kill die kill too and shock shock into stopping but doesn't stop, saying die kill die leaving rooms blowing up blowing up blocks shooting self burning self shooting own family or strangers strangers in street on the news and I switch off I switch I switch off but now I can't and I'm glad glad no more waiting so do it kill me do kill me now and get it over over get it over.

CLAUDE   I haven't come for that.

VIVIAN   Not?

CLAUDE   Not going to kill anyone else. Just came to see my
father. Thought he'd be glad afterwards that he saw me
once more first. Not happening till this evening so there's
been the day to fill with last things. You've nothing to be
frightened of.

MICK   Claude, what stupid idea is this? I'm not angry about
the money. You can always earn money. If you live to be
as old as me you could earn all that money a hundred
times over. You could give it away each time, what about
that, and start again. That would do more good, wouldn't it?
And in your life there would be happy times. In everyone's life. You would love someone almost certainly. Even
without children, even with everything the way it is and
getting worse you could be happy at times. There are always
moments.

CLAUDE   Better be going.

MICK   Going? No, wait, let me make it clear.

CLAUDE   (*getting up*) Time I went.

MICK   No, sit, stay there a moment. In the chair.

CLAUDE *sits down.*

Looking at me. Your mother's eyes. My hair. I had hair like
that, Claude, but longer was the thing then.

CLAUDE   (*getting up*) Easier if I go now. Goodbye.

MICK   Wait.

CLAUDE   What?

MICK   Something I forgot to tell you. We saw a sparrow. Do
you know what I mean? It's a bird. A sparrow.

CLAUDE   Must have been nice for you.

MICK   It was, it was. I wish you'd seen it.

CLAUDE   Goodbye then.

MICK   It must still be about somewhere. If you keep your eyes open –

CLAUDE *goes.*

Claude, Claude, not like that, don't go, tell me when you'll come and see me.

VIVIAN   If we look look out of the window we may see him may see him going.

MICK   I can't see so far down.

VIVIAN   I'll open open the window.

MICK   Yes, yes, open it.

VIVIAN *opens the window.*

VIVIAN   Oh the smell.

MICK   Never mind, never mind, look out. Is that him? It's someone isn't it ? Is it Claude? I can't see.

VIVIAN   The smoke hurts my eyes hurts – yes it's him.

MICK   There he goes then, there . . . I can't see him.

VIVIAN   Yes yes I can I can just just I can just see him still still just –

MICK   Still?

VIVIAN   No he's no no he's gone.

MICK   Shut the window. Spray your stuff about.

VIVIAN *shuts the window but stays looking out.*

VIVIAN   Look more look more flames.

MICK   Not from him?

VIVIAN   Not what not from him?

MICK   No, I'm sorry. What a silly mistake. I thought for a
moment he was –

VIVIAN   No no no from a block a block another block on fire.

MICK   Spray the spray about. I've a headache again.

VIVIAN *sprays oxygen.*

VIVIAN   Have a drink let's have a drink drink of water.

MICK   Stupid boy.

VIVIAN *pours a small glass of water each from the jug.*

VIVIAN   Though the park the park is mostly rows of cottages
mud a little little grass if you like we could go this spring this
spring we could go this spring to see see to see the grass and
flowers flowers in the park.

MICK   I'm too old.

VIVIAN   No no not too not too old because I would come too I
would come and it would be an adventure for us to go an
adventure to go together and enjoy enjoy ourselves in the
park.

MICK   You'd better move your things into this room.

VIVIAN   Yes I will I will and I'll get some new puzzles new
harder harder puzzles for you though I can't do the sky on
the big jigsaw with all those blue blue bits of sky – as if sky
was blue – all look the same but you're so good at it. We can
do that we can do that tonight and listen to music. We'll see
news news of Claude on telly we'll see news of Claude.

MICK   Yes I think his death might get a mention. Switch it on.

42

The Judge's Wife

Characters

JUDGE, 60s
CAROLINE, his wife, about 60
BARBARA, Caroline's sister, 60s
PEG, the Judge's maid, 20s
VERNON WARREN, a young man
MICHAEL WARREN, his brother
WARREN'S MOTHER, 50s

The Judge's Wife was first transmitted on BBC 2, on 2 October 1972 with the following cast:

JUDGE	*Sebastian Shaw*
CAROLINE	*Rachel Kempson*
BARBARA	*Valerie White*
PEG	*Evin Crowley*
MICHEAL WARREN	*Anthony Andrews*
VERNON WARREN	
WARREN'S MOTHER	*Grace Dolan*

Directed by James Fearman

An old man, the JUDGE, *is lying shot dead in a wood.*
The JUDGE *and a young man,* MICHAEL WARREN, *are standing in the*
wood. WARREN *shoots the* JUDGE. *The* JUDGE *is lying dead exactly as*
before. A car stops at the edge of the wood. The JUDGE *and* WARREN *get*
out and walk into the wood. Then an exact repeat of them standing in
the wood, WARREN *shooting the* JUDGE, *the* JUDGE *lying dead.*
A close-up of the JUDGE, *alive, in his wig.*

JUDGE   Every criminal is a revolutionary. And every revolutionary is a criminal. For they both act in defiance of laws
that protect us, protect our property, protect what we in this
society have chosen to be. And whether a man who comes
against the forces of law and order presents himself to us as
a criminal or as a revolutionary is irrelevant. In either case
he is challenging our society. And he must take the heavy
consequences. For our society is upheld by force and we
should not be afraid to admit it. The forces of law and order
are stronger than those of revolt and we will not hesitate to
use our strength.

We have police to do what we want done. They are
armed with truncheons, dogs, horses, cars, gas sometimes
and sometimes guns. If necessary we have the army, and
there is no limit to the force that could in theory be brought
to bear against the country's enemies. To eliminate the
entire population would be impractical but not impossible
and goes to show that it is not strength we lack. So why do we
pretend? Why do we not say plainly that we will use any
means necessary to keep things the way they are? We will
never be intimidated. Your violence will be met by violence
and we are stronger than you.

A close-up of VERNON WARREN, *the accused. His face is calm and*
doesn't change while the JUDGE *speaks.*

Vernon Warren, you have attempted to overthrow the
established institutions of this realm and you have urged
others to do so. That you have failed in this shameful enter-

prise is due to your ineptitude and the great vigilance of the police. But are you to be rewarded for this failure with a light sentence so that you may rest for a while at the state's expense perfecting your schemes and try to do better a second time?

A close-up of the JUDGE.

No, you must be punished according to your intention.

WARREN'S MOTHER *is standing in her kitchen. She is in her fifties, shapeless, lined, tired. Tears are running down her face.*

A close-up of PEG, *an Irish girl in her twenties, her hair tied back off her face, wearing an apron.*

PEG   That was a heavy sentence, sir.

PEG, *the* JUDGE *and* CAROLINE, *the* JUDGE*'s wife, are in the hall of the house. The* JUDGE *has just come in.* CAROLINE *has come to meet him.* PEG *stands further off, by the door to the kitchen.*

CAROLINE   Go, go back to the kitchen at once. How dare you speak to the Judge like that?

JUDGE   We shall have no more Irish girls.

The JUDGE *is standing in the bathroom by the bath, which is running.* CAROLINE *undresses him. He is completely passive. He stands naked, fat, old, defenceless.*

WARREN *is sitting at a kitchen table with uneaten food. After a moment he looks round, half draws a gun out of his pocket, slips it back. His* MOTHER *comes in. She has been crying. She puts her arm round* WARREN *and he leans his head against her.*

PEG *is banging veal escalopes in the kitchen, and goes on banging while* CAROLINE *talks.*

CAROLINE   You're very lucky he managed to keep his temper. I hope you realise that. The Judge is exhausted. He has been listening for twelve days. I'm sure you never listen for five minutes. His summing up took fourteen hours. Could you speak intelligently for fourteen hours? At a time like this he needs our support and comfort. Try to make up for your insolence by cooking a perfect dinner and all may yet be forgiven.

PEG *goes on banging.*

The JUDGE *is lying in the bath, his eyes closed. The phone rings, off. He opens his eyes.*

CAROLINE   (*lifting the phone*) Yes? (*She listens a moment, closing her eyes, then puts the receiver down.*)

The JUDGE *is wide-eyed in the bath.* CAROLINE *comes in, holds out a large towel for him. He gets out. She wraps him in it. They start out of the bathroom. He slips on the wet floor and almost falls.*

JUDGE   Damn your eyes, Caroline, be more careful.

The JUDGE *and* CAROLINE*'s bedroom: twin beds, a dressing-table, a small portable TV on the table. We can see the screen but only as one of many things in the room, not close up. The sound is low but audible. The* JUDGE*'s clothes are laid out on the bed.*

TV   At the Old Bailey today Vernon Warren, leader of the –

The JUDGE *turns the sound right down. The TV shows stills of* VERNON WARREN *and the* JUDGE, *film of demonstrators with placards, arrests, scuffles, general violence. This is never close up, but in a small intense corner of the large, still bedroom where the* JUDGE *goes on slowly getting dressed, not looking at the TV.* CAROLINE *helps but he is more active now and sometimes pushes her off irritably, tying his own tie. When he is dressed he goes out of the room. When he has gone* CAROLINE *looks at the TV but it is on to a different item.*

BARBARA *meets the* JUDGE *on the stairs. He starts, then indifferent, cold, nods impatiently. She stops and looks at him hard with dislike, watches him go down, then goes on up.*

BARBARA *and* CAROLINE *are in the bedroom.* BARBARA*'s face is in profile. We see* CAROLINE *full-face in the mirror of the dressing-table, and the back of her head. She is sitting at the dressing-table making up her face. They are sisters and both about sixty. They have similar faces but* BARBARA*, with no make-up, short untidy hair, and indifferent clothes, is an old woman.* CAROLINE*, as she makes up, looks far younger, bland, without character.*

BARBARA   Do you always agree with what he does?

CAROLINE   Oh yes.

BARBARA   I know Warren had to be found guilty. But weren't you all shocked by the sentence?

CAROLINE   Shocked? by the sentence? I was shocked by the crimes.

BARBARA   Yes, Laurence said he was shocked by the crimes.

CAROLINE   I am his wife, Barbara. You don't seem to understand about marriage.

BARBARA   If you thought he was wrong would you say so? Or does his wife keep quiet?

CAROLINE   Sentencing is his job. It's a very technical matter. I wouldn't expect to know if he did it wrong. Some other expert might. My job is looking after him.

BARBARA   Are you frightened of him?

CAROLINE   What a funny idea, Barbara. Are you?

BARBARA   What would he do to you if you said what you really think?

CAROLINE   But I really think he's absolutely right. Don't start on politics, please darling, or he won't sleep tonight and nor will I.

BARBARA *turns away.*

CAROLINE *looks at herself steadily and miserably. She smiles radiantly, holds it for a moment, then lets it go and stares at herself as before.*

The living-room.

The JUDGE *is striking matches and putting them out between his finger and thumb. The phone rings. He answers with a grunt. After a moment he hangs up. He sits impassive.*

CAROLINE, *holding a small dog, is watching the* JUDGE. BARBARA *is also watching him.*
He starts striking matches again.

CAROLINE   I don't see why we don't get the police to tap the phone and find out where he is and deal with him in the proper way.

WARREN *comes out of phone-box, gets into cab (the same one as at the beginning) and drives off.*

Back in the living-room.

CAROLINE   I've always said our number should be ex-directory. We get these endless calls from cranks of all sorts.

JUDGE   I like to hear how I'm hated. I wouldn't be doing my job if everyone liked me.

BARBARA   You've gone too far this time, Laurence. I used to think you were an old fool but meant well. Now I think you're bloody dangerous.

JUDGE   (*to* CAROLINE) Tell your sister that a plain old spinster doesn't make herself more interesting by being rude. And give me another whisky larger than the last one. And tell that slut in the kitchen that last night's dinner was so incompetent that I suspect her of deliberate sabotage.

BARBARA   If you want to hear how you're hated you should get her to tell you some time.

49

CAROLINE   Barbara, you haven't been talking to the cook?

BARBARA   The number of sharp knives she has in there I'm surprised you can sleep.

CAROLINE   (*giving the* JUDGE *whisky*) Barbara, how can you?

JUDGE   The good girl is angry with me for being so horrid to the pretty young man. There's no death sentence unfortunately. No one is being flogged. Do you think your whining, Barbara, has any effect on me? I know your namby-pamby politics. Do you think I care if five thousand people are out tonight rioting in protest at my sentence? Ha, I only wish I had made it double.

WARREN *is driving the car with the* JUDGE *beside him. The car pulls up by the edge of the wood.* WARREN *and the* JUDGE *get out exactly as before, the whole sequence being repeated till the* JUDGE *is lying dead.*

The JUDGE, CAROLINE, *and* BARBARA *are sitting at the dinner-table. There is soup in their bowls but only* CAROLINE *has started to eat.*

JUDGE   I shall retire to a remote island.

BARBARA   I wish you would.

JUDGE   I will. The west of Scotland. Guillemots. Cormorants. Shag.

CAROLINE   There are things one would miss. Not people perhaps.

JUDGE   There's no shortage of whisky in Scotland.

CAROLINE   I wonder if Harrods would deliver?

BARBARA   In fact, you'll dodder on till you're eighty and completely senile with all your judgements reversed by the Court of Appeal.

JUDGE   Do you know that's never happened to me yet?

BARBARA   It will now. They'll halve Warren's sentence.

JUDGE   My judgements stand.

CAROLINE   Which island have you in mind, Laurence?

BARBARA   Laurence, I don't defend violence. I am a pacifist, as you know very well.

JUDGE   More fool you. What are people that you should mind them being killed? Look about you when you walk down the street. Such faces. Which of them would stop to save you? They would see you dead, Barbara, and me, and Caroline, and anyone except each his own little family, and most murders, of course, are precisely of husbands and wives or gassing the children. I don't know why death should be an issue. Think of the deaths on the road. If cars are worth all the slaughter almost any cause however bad must be worth a few people dead.

BARBARA   I'm only saying that I don't defend violence but I still don't think that Warren's crimes, though I agree they are crimes of violence, though I have every sympathy with the victims –

CAROLINE   Whatever you may say about Peg, she does make delicious vichyssoise.

JUDGE   Will you not interrupt me?

CAROLINE   I think we will spoil our appetite if we talk about work at dinner.

JUDGE   Spoil our appetite? Who has an appetite for this muck? Call the girl in.

CAROLINE   Ah no, it's delicious soup, isn't it Barbara?

BARBARA   Yes the soup's fine, Laurence, we can talk and drink our soup.

JUDGE   We can't drink this. It tastes of nothing but salt.

BARBARA   You put that in yourself.

51

CAROLINE   Let me taste.

JUDGE   Take the stuff away.

CAROLINE   Why you've put in far too much salt, you silly old thing. Have mine.

JUDGE   Call the girl in here. I shall call her. Peg is it? Peg. Peg.

CAROLINE   This is your fault, Barbara. It is. I've warned and warned you not to criticise.

PEG *comes in.*

JUDGE   What is this? What do you call it?

PEG   Vichyssoise soup, sir.

JUDGE   It is sea water, Peg.

CAROLINE   The Judge has accidentally put in a little too much salt.

JUDGE   And without the salt what would it be? It would be Irish bog water. I know you mad Irish live off potatoes but I don't want potato and bog water served up as soup in my house. Take it away. Take it all away.

BARBARA   I should like to finish mine.

JUDGE   I said take it away.

PEG *clears away the soup and goes out.*
The phone rings.
The JUDGE *doesn't get up.*
CAROLINE *sits looking down at the table.*
BARBARA *watches the* JUDGE.
The phone goes on ringing.
The JUDGE *gets up suddenly, picks up the receiver and at once puts it down again.*

BARBARA   Why don't you retire? I think that's a good idea.

JUDGE   And live alone on an island with this cow? Don't think while you eat or you won't sleep. Don't talk while you sleep or you won't eat. Don't think while you talk.

CAROLINE   This case has taken it out of you.

JUDGE   And why shouldn't it? I was trying my right to exist, don't you know that? Warren is what is happening to us. His speeches and pamphlets are stirring this country up to a new idea of what is possible. It is for me to show that it is not possible. To put out this fire with my hands.

PEG *comes in with a tray of food.*

What's this?

PEG   Escalope of veal, sir. And I hope it chokes you.

CAROLINE   Peg! No, no, Laurence, don't hurt her.

The JUDGE *hasn't moved towards* PEG. *He is just looking at her.*

Peg, run back to the kitchen.

JUDGE   Have you ever tried to poison me?

PEG   (*still putting the food on the table*) I've thought of it many times. I'll be leaving now and I won't come back again. I won't be working for anyone at all. It was my mistake ever to come to England. I'm going home tomorrow.

CAROLINE   Go away, Peg, go back to the kitchen.

PEG   (*to the* JUDGE) Not till I tell you what I think of you. You remind me of a toad I saw one time run over by a tractor. It was sitting there like you swelled up and ugly and then there was nothing left of it at all.

The JUDGE *gets into the car with* WARREN. WARREN *is driving the car. The whole sequence is repeated exactly as before until the* JUDGE *is lying dead in the wood.*

The food is uneaten on the plates.

The JUDGE, CAROLINE *and* BARBARA *are sitting in the living-room, silently, with drinks. There are footsteps in the hall. The front door bangs shut.*

CAROLINE   I wonder what she's stolen.

BARBARA   You can't be surprised.

CAROLINE   I'm always surprised when people don't like me. I do like to be liked. How nice it would be to be liked by everyone.

JUDGE   Our duty is to be hated if necessary.

BARBARA   But you do stir up such ill feeling. You go out of your way. I think Vernon Warren's movement would simply die out if left to itself and reforms would come as they do in England slowly but surely and without any violence. But you're making him a martyr. Every worker, every black, every student thinks tonight he might even die for Warren and quite a few will feel the same tomorrow and some actually will die for him.

JUDGE   Do you think so?

BARBARA   Didn't you see the size of the demonstration? And that was just what happened spontaneously, the few people outside the court. They'll organise something big at the weekend. You are so stupid, Laurence.

JUDGE   Hundreds of them will be arrested. And given heavy sentences.

BARBARA   And then?

The phone rings.
The JUDGE *answers, listens.*

JUDGE   I'm not afraid, you know.

He hangs up.

54

BARBARA   You should talk to Thomas.

CAROLINE   We don't want to talk to our children, thank you very much. We do our best to avoid that sort of thing.

BARBARA   He agrees with me I'm sure.

JUDGE   I don't know what sort of socialist Thomas is. He's as plump as any conservative I know. He does just manage to use state schools and that's his greatest sacrifice so far. I think socialist is something he calls himself to annoy me. But I'm not interested enough to be annoyed. I would rather not have had children. I would rather not have been born. I would rather the apes had stayed in the trees.

WARREN *is sitting in the parked car in the dark.*
Back to the living-room, as before, but now CAROLINE *has a tray of coffee and is pouring it out.*

CAROLINE   Will coffee keep you awake?

JUDGE   I shall never sleep again. Give me the coffee.

CAROLINE   He keeps me awake too, I'm not allowed to sleep if he can't sleep.

BARBARA   I seem to think when you were young, Laurence, you weren't so hateful. Spiky, yes, but Caroline and I liked spiky men. You couldn't get hold of them too easily. You weren't very bright about politics but you certainly weren't this right-wing buffoon. Jack the Ripper of the Queen's Bench. I lived abroad so much I lost track. But even twenty years ago you were quite ordinary. It's since then. Did power corrupt like it's supposed to?

JUDGE   Go away Barbara. I've had enough. Should we all be kind? You are lukewarm and will be vomited. There are two camps, Barbara, mine and theirs. Either you are with, or you are against.

BARBARA   I do dislike that silly way of talking.

JUDGE   You know nothing. You only see yourself. You never married. You never lived. You will die without having been born.

BARBARA   I never married you and I would kill myself if I was in Caroline's position now.

CAROLINE   You were never asked to marry him.

BARBARA   Yes, I was.

CAROLINE   I don't believe you and we're too old now for jealousy.

JUDGE   I asked her and it's lucky she said no because I don't like antiseptic mouthwash, I like a drink.

The phone rings. The JUDGE *lets it ring while he pours himself a drink, then answers.*

JUDGE   I should like very much to see you face to face. I should like to see which of us was frightened. (*He listens a bit more then hangs up.*)

BARBARA   None of us has done all we might have done.

JUDGE   I have done everything possible. You haven't, no. Be maudlin, yes, it suits you, Barbara.

CAROLINE   When was it you asked her to marry you?

JUDGE   (*to* BARBARA) When this country runs with blood I shall go down fighting. I hope to see you killed in the crossfire.

CAROLINE   More coffee, Barbara?

JUDGE   Caroline, I'm going out for a walk.

CAROLINE   A walk?

JUDGE   Yes, and without a scarf.

CAROLINE.   Will you take the dog?

56

JUDGE   No.

CAROLINE   He needs to go. Peg isn't here to do it.

JUDGE   I do not want the dog. Let him piss on the carpet.

BARBARA   I shouldn't walk about too much, Laurence. It may not be safe. You aren't very popular.

JUDGE   I am unpopular because I choose to be. If I wanted to be popular, how I would be loved.

He goes out.
BARBARA *and* CAROLINE *are sitting side by side on the sofa in silence.*

Another road.
The JUDGE *walks on.*
As before, the JUDGE *gets into the car with* WARREN *and the sequence is repeated until the* JUDGE *lies dead in the wood.*
A still of the JUDGE *lying dead in the wood on the front page of a newspaper.*
It is the next day. CAROLINE *is sitting on the sofa. She wears a dressing-gown. Her hair is unbrushed, her face crumpled.*
BARBARA *is standing.*
They are two old women.

CAROLINE   You think he deserved it.

BARBARA *shakes her head.*

He tried to deserve it. It was his way of committing suicide.

BARBARA *looks up, interested, but says nothing.*

Because what else is there to do? We're dying out. If you're a pig you might as well cut your own throat as run round the yard squealing. Why did Laurence turn out so horrible? He was promising. He had all the right ideas, you used to think. But he lost touch. He lost his grip. He wasn't just a right-wing bigot, he was a parody of a right-wing bigot. Didn't you think so? Didn't you think he rather overdid it?

57

Or did you fall for the whole thing? Did you really? Did you never suspect? No? I thought you would, of all people. You're not so bright as you and I think. Sneering to yourself, 'poor Caroline, stuck with a senile fascist'. You really did? He was very good, wasn't he, he could have been a great actor. 'This is pure parody, Laurence,' I would say. 'Nobody will believe a word of it.' He said, 'Don't worry Caroline. Anything I'm fool enough to say, they'll be fool enough to believe.' Even you. He had to make himself worse and worse because at first we would think he was shocking and next day we'd meet someone at dinner saying far more stupid and aggressive things. Unless they were pretending too of course, unless every reactionary fool in the country is playing at it, it may all be a vast plot. Perhaps when we rode our ponies in Hyde Park, two little girls with ringlets, we were pretending, do you think so? We came home to tea and mama's hands were cold and smooth. She was never the one who cleaned the floors. 'But why', you're about to ask me. Do you find you don't understand your Laurence quite so well? Some things he didn't have to pretend. He liked whisky, that came easily, and he despised you. He did despise your weak liberal slop just as he said. Because he might have been like you. He was. He didn't go to fight in Spain. He didn't have to leave the Communist Party over Hungary because he had never joined it. He lived on day after day. Then the crisis came. He couldn't sleep. Everyone in middle age wonders what on earth they've done with their life. Then they carry on. But he stopped. He lay there night after night. The oppressed people were rising all over the world he said and he found himself on the wrong side. And what could he do now? Could he extricate himself from his career, his large house, the money his father left him, the whisky? No, he had to admit, no. He was cut off forever from people who suffered. He had become the enemy. He loathed himself. He said he would commit suicide. And then at a brilliant stroke he saw what he could do for other people. He could be the enemy. He saw that violence was necessary but he couldn't have brought himself to be violent. Comfort makes the conscience tender. It had to be the oppressed who rose up and he could never be one of them. But he could help them to revolt by making them hate him. He could live out his way of life but more extremely. He could help make the establishment so despicable that everyone would see it had to go. He could use his power so unjustly that someone would be forced to take it away from him. He wouldn't kill but he could be killed. He could give his life for the revolution.

So what he had to do was make himself hated by everybody. Sometimes by me. It hasn't been easy. I can't say we've had a happy life. But that you see was what he was doing.

BARBARA   I don't believe you, Caroline. I think you're making it up.

CAROLINE *doesn't react. She sits impassive.*
BARBARA *looking at her. A song silence.*

The JUDGE'*s house from across the road, as before.*
The JUDGE *is leaving, going with* WARREN, *exactly as before, repeating the sequence ending with the* JUDGE *lying dead in the wood.*

Notes to help your reading

The notes in this edition are intended to serve the needs of overseas students as well as those of British-born users.

Seagulls

4 *Harvard*: a famous and highly respected American university.

5 *Marks and Spencer's*: a chain of British department stores.

6 *Flash Gordon*: an American comic strip hero.

7 *repressing*: hiding their feelings.

9 *nuclear physics*: commonly thought of as the most complex, fast developing and advanced area of science, dealing with difficult questions about the physical universe.
    energy resource: source of electrical power.

10 *inflation*: a rise in prices caused by increased cost of production or increase in people's wages.
    protecting the whale: the organisation Greenpeace has made this a major issue in the context of the international protection of endangered species.

17 *agency*: an organisation which handles bookings and conditions of employment on behalf of several performers.

19 *scientific guarantee*: proof that Valery's ability is not fake.
    slink: creep.

20 *guck*: an American word for mess.
    human potential: what it may be possible for humans to achieve.

21 *Chinese wisdom*: famous for being expressed in short puzzling sayings or stories.
    lit: settled.

22 *con trick*: fake (a confidence trick).

Not Not Not Not Not Enough Oxygen

24 *contemporary*: belonging to the same period of time. Here 'contemporary' means the real period in which the play is performed.

intercom: a microphone and receiver through which a visitor at the locked front door of the block of flats can speak to a resident.

smoggy: fog formed by car exhaust fumes.

25 *local authority*: the regional government responsible for funding local services such as housing. This one is providing faster lifts rather than more oxygen for the flats.

the park authority: the local authority for 'the park' area outside 'the Londons'.

28 *A daily dress*: it is unclear whether this means 'a dress for each day' or 'a dress for just daily use'.

29 *in the jam*: the traffic jam seems to be continuous.

fanatics: Mick's word for those people who take violent protest action against the authorities.

30 *a sparrow*: a common bird in London and other cities before 2010.

elimination: pigeons seem to have all been killed by the authorities.

31 *blackbird, starling, bluetit*: common garden birds before 2010.

32 *How can I get a doctor?*: Mick does not know how to get a doctor.

34 *no sewage problem*: some blocks seem to have problems with toilets that don't work.

mind tickles: the newspapers have puzzles to 'tickle' the minds of readers.

relinquished: gave up.

35 *which I have just mentioned, I think*: he hasn't, has he?

exemption: permission to be different. Abortion appears to

61

be compulsory if you get pregnant without a licence to have a baby.

36 *one of the epidemic areas*: areas where disease spreads quickly affecting everyone.

the lottery: the poor put their names down to be drawn by chance and win a licence for permission to have a baby.

37 *walking about*: i.e. in the open spaces, beyond the control of the authorities.

38 *little box*: i.e. this room.

The Judge's Wife

45 *intimidated*: frightened by threatening behaviour.

institutions: codes of behaviour upheld by laws, for example, respect for ownership of property, acceptance of the authority of those in power.

46 *ineptitude*: inability to carry out intentions.

vigilance: alertness to threats.

veal escalopes: steaks of veal (young beef) which have been made tender before cooking by being beaten with a wooden hammer.

47 *summing up*: the Judge's guidance to the jury at the end of a trial before the verdict is given.

insolence: rudeness.

placards: signs held by demonstrators to say what they think in a short slogan.

indifferent: not showing any feelings.

48 *indifferent*: unremarkable.

49 *radiantly*: brightly, as though for public show.

impassive: neither moving nor showing any emotion.

ex-directory: not available in the telephone directory.

incompetent: unskilled to the point of failure.

sabotage: as a protest, deliberately damaging something so that it won't work.

50 *namby-pamby*: soft, too weak.

Guillemots, Cormorants, Shag: birds common in the Western Isles.

Harrods: expensive London department store.

51 *vichyssoise*: creamy soup of leeks and potatoes served chilled.

52 *bog water*: Ireland is famous for its peat bogs.

53 *trying*: judging at the trial.

54 *movement*: political group.

spontaneously: without previous planning.

55 *Spiky*: having a sharp tongue or a bitter sarcastic wit.

buffoon: fool.

Jack the Ripper: famous nineteenth-century rapist and murderer.

power currupt: from the saying, 'Power corrupts; absolute power corrupts absolutely'.

lukewarm and will be vomited: insulting way of calling Barbara's attitude a weak one.

56 *maudlin*: miserably sad in a self-pitying way.

57 *bigot*: someone with deeply rooted prejudices who deliberately displays them.

58 *poor Caroline, stuck with a senile fascist*: Caroline is imagining that Barbara is sneering to herself and thinking these words.

senile: mentally disorientated through old age.

fascist: someone who believes in dictatorship and total state control. The term usually implies extreme right-wing views, including racism.

parody: a weak and unsuccessful copy.

reactionary: someone who wants to keep things as they are and reacts against suggestions of change.

He didn't go to fight in Spain: During the Spanish Civil War (1936–39) many British socialists, such as the writer George Orwell, went to fight with the Republicans against the Fascist army of General Franco.

leave the Communist Party over Hungary: some members of

the British Communist Party resigned their membership when the Soviet army invaded Hungary in 1956. The Russian government thought that the Hungarian regime was getting too liberal for a communist country under its control.

Writing essays

Many of the written assignments in the next section, 'Coursework assignments', ask you to write an essay. It may be helpful to consider how you can plan your essay in several stages.

It can be helpful to discuss with others your ideas about the subject of the essay, then jot down the points you want to write about.

Use the notes you made in your Reading log where these are relevant to the subject of your essay.

Taking the example of the essay question in Assignment 2 on page 67, collect relevant points together in a topic web like this:

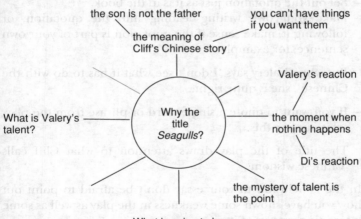

Now go through the play selecting passages you want to discuss in relation to each point. Note several different interpretations, if you can see several, of each passage. Decide which you favour yourself and why.

Plan a flow chart to represent the structure of your essay in general outline:
– the puzzle of the play's title
– the meaning of the Chinese story
– the turning point of the play
– similarities of the plot with Cliff's story
– the suggestion of the ending of the play
– conclusion: possible meanings of the title.

You will want to quote certain lines of the play to demonstrate a point.
– Use a colon to indicate that you are to quote.
– Use quotation marks to indicate the start and finish of the quotation.
– Lay out the quotation so that it is separate from your own writing.
– Set out the quotation just as it is in the book.
– Make your own writing leading into the quotation, or following it, make sense if the quotation is part of your own sentence, for example:

But when Valery says 'I don't see what it has to do with the Chinese', she is quite right.

– If you want to quote a single word or phrase from the play, set it out like this:

The title of the play draws attention to what Cliff calls 'Chinese wisdom'.

In the conclusion to your essay don't be afraid to point out how you have shown some weakness in the play as well as some interesting aspects of it.

Coursework assignments

The following suggestions for oral and written activities are intended to help you to clarify and develop your responses to the plays. They are particularly appropriate for oral and written assessment in GCSE English or English Literature. They provide opportunities:
- to take part in pair discussions
- to take part in group performances
- to produce situations for oral assessment
- to write imaginative extensions of the plays
- to write critical, analytic essays.

You are not expected to attempt every assignment. Choose those which most interest you and provide you with the best variety of oral and written activities.

Seagulls

Themes for talking and writing

Assignment 1

In pairs, summarise what you have been shown about each of the three characters in the play before and after the failed performance.

Explore your opinion about each of these characters on reflection at the end of the play.

Assignment 2

The title of the play draws attention to the story illustrating Chinese wisdom that Cliff tells on pages 20–21. What is the moral of this little story? Cliff says 'I wonder if that's relevant at all?' Do you think it is?

Explain your answer in an essay with carefully selected quotes.

Assignment 3

With a partner, choose a section of dialogue to rehearse and perform. Be prepared to say why you have chosen it.

Try performing it in at least two different ways to show two different interpretations of the characters' motives and feelings. Then decide on one interpretation to perform for the rest of the class. Before your performance write down what you are trying to show and why. Refer to other parts of the play in your explanation.

Evaluate how successful you have been by asking for comments on what your performance has suggested. Then add a written evaluation to your writing about how successfully you put across your intentions.

Imaginative and personal response

You may find it helpful to refer back to 'How to write plays' on page xxiv.

Assignment 1

Valery develops a new performance which Cliff comes to see.

Write three scenes about this:
scene 1 – Cliff and Valery before the show;
scene 2 – the performance;
scene 3 – Cliff and Valery after the show.

Assignment 2

Di says to Valery, 'You're one of the first of a new species of person'. Imagine that in the future all ordinary people have developed a special ability similar to Valery's.

Write a story set in the future about a family disagreement based on characters in your own family who all have this special ability. How could they use it in this situation? How will you resolve the disagreement?

Assignment 3

The play ends with Valery 'watching things move'. What does this suggest to you? Discuss this with a partner.

Assignment 4

After the end of the play Valery begins writing again to one of her little girls, who is now grown up.

Write the sequence of two or more letters that they send to each other in the months following the end of the play.

Assignment 5

Cliff writes a report for an American magazine on his visit to this performance.

Re-read carefully Cliff's final conversation with Valery, then write the article you think he might write.

Assignment 6

A 'housewife' discovers that she has an amazing special ability and decides to perform on stage as a career.

Record a magazine interview with her about her life, at a time when her powers are coming to be doubted.

Assignment 7

Imagine a TV performer whose famous trick goes wrong one night.

Write the performer's diary account of what happened and its implications.

Critical and analytical response

You may find it helpful to look at 'Writing essays' on page 65.

Assignment 1

Do you think that this is a good play? Using the two headings, 'strengths' and 'weaknesses', list how the author has used the following techniques to achieve what you feel to be the play's strengths and weaknesses:
- use of dialogue
- speech characteristics of an individual; for example Valery's claim that she has no skills except being able to run a home
- characterisation; for example Valery is presented as just an ordinary person by giving her no special mental preparation for her performances – she just has a cup of tea instead
- live dramatic effects; for example Valery's failure to move the knob that sets off the rocket
- structure of the scenes; for example two dialogues before the climax and two after it
- development of a theme; for example Valery's special powers are revealed to the audience, shown as a failure, then shown to have changed.

Now write a critical evaluation of the play being careful to illustrate your points by quoting from the play.

Assignment 2

Look back at Assignment 1 on page 67. Now plan and write a study of two characters in the play showing:
(a) how each of them has been developed as a character. Have you seen different aspects of either by the end of the play?
(b) how the characters have changed in their relationship with each other.

   You could chose to study Di and Valery or Cliff and Valery. You will need to make notes on the moments when the writer reveals new aspects of a character, and on the scenes where they change in their relationship with each other.

Assignment 3

Make notes in answer to each of the following questions:
(a) What would you say is the main theme of the play?
   – Is it about the nature of talent in an ordinary person?
   – Is it about relationships?
   – Is it about greed? Or desire?
(b) What is the writer asking the audience to think about? Why has she given the play this title?
(c) What techniques does the writer use to make the audience think at different moments in the play; for example Valery's long speech on pages 10–11.
(d) What are your responses to the writer's development of her themes? What has the play led you to think about these themes?

Now plan an essay in which you explore how Caryl Churchill has made you think about the themes of the play.

71

Not Not Not Not Not Enough Oxygen

Themes for talking and writing

Assignment 1

Write ten questions you would like to ask the author of this play.

Ask a partner to role-play the author's answers to your questions. Then swop notes so that you answer your partner's questions.

Assignment 2

With a partner, choose a passage of dialogue to prepare for performance.

Try performing your lines in at least two different ways, exploring different interpretations of the character's feelings. Decide on a final way of saying your lines for a performance for the rest of the class.

Assignment 3

You are planning to write a story set in the future forty years from now. Discuss with a partner changes which you might show in the following:
- dress
- speech
- where people live
- living conditions
- nature and the environment
- entertainment
- transport
- medical services
- the evidence of state control
- forms of social protest.

Assignment 4

The population of the world is increasing so fast that many experts are concerned for the future. Problems of food supply, water purification, pollution and housing space are bound to increase as the Earth's human population continues to grow.

In a group imagine that you are the future single government of the planet Earth and list possible ways of controlling population growth. Then discuss which measures you would find acceptable if you were the government of the future.

Imaginative and personal response

Assignment 1

Mick and Vivian have just switched off the television news which has announced Claude's death. Write the dialogue of their discussion.

You will need to have noticed their individual speech patterns and to have considered how they will react, based on your understanding of their attitudes in the play so far. (See also 'How to write plays' on page xxiv.)

Assignment 2

Describe the changes in the environment in the year 2010 and the way they affect the people in the play. Say how you think these changes might be avoided by action now.

Critical and analytical response

Assignment 1

Mick says to Vivian, before Claude arrives, 'You're still young. You can help us speak to each other' (page 28). What do you notice about the speech differences between the characters of different ages?

Write about the way the author shows you differences between characters by their individual ways of speaking and use of words.

Assignment 2

Mick and Vivian seem to have similar feelings about the world of 2010, but the other characters mentioned in the play (including Claude's mother, and Alexander and his wife) have different responses. Make notes on the attitudes underlying the decisions made by each of the characters mentioned in the play.

Mick says of Alexander, 'He was always too full of ideals' (page 35), but Vivian says a little later that he is a 'fanatic'. Which of the characters would you say is an idealist and which a fanatic? Which attitude do you think would be closest to your own if you lived in the world of the play? What do you think Caryl Churchill is saying in this play about the difference between idealists and fanatics?

Use your notes to write an account of the range of attitudes indicated in the play, saying how they are revealed and what you think of each of them. Conclude by saying what you think is Caryl Churchill's point of view about accepting or changing society, as expressed in this play.

Assignment 3

How would you describe the relationship between Mick and Vivian? In what ways does Claude disappoint his father's expectations ? How does Mick react ? Do his reactions change?

Using your answers to these questions, write an account of the state of relationships in 2010, giving your opinion on what you think Caryl Churchill is suggesting.

The Judge's Wife

Themes for talking and writing

Assignment 1

Explain to a partner what Caroline is suggesting in her final speech. Discuss together whether you believe her or Barbara. Look back over the play to make sure you can support your view.

Assignment 2

The play's title draws attention to the role of the wife. Discuss with a partner what Caryl Churchill has shown you about the Judge's wife and what you think of this. What would you have done in the position of the wife in this play? If you disagreed with the Judge about an aspect of his work with whom would you feel it right to discuss your views?

Assignment 3

Discuss how far you think wives and husbands of celebrities should support the views and actions of their more famous partners. If they disagree with their partners, what form should their expression of disagreement take? For example, should they try to persuade their partner? What should they say to
(a) their own parents?
(b) their friends?
(c) their partner's friends?
(d) press interviewers?

Assignment 4

In a group, make a list of different people who want to change some aspect of the way those in power do things at present.

These may be people who work for change locally or nationally or internationally. Discuss any action they may have taken to help other people or to draw attention to something they feel strongly about. How successful do you feel they have been? How far do you think such people should go to promote their cause?

Now try to group those people as fanatics or not fanatics. List their names under each heading.

Imaginative and personal response

Assignment 1

Write two newspaper reports of the Judge's death, one for a newspaper that Caroline might read and another for a newspaper that Vernon might read.

Assignment 2

Write a story in which an employee who is mistreated gets his/her own back on the employer, but give your story a twist in the end.

Assignment 3

In the past, a number of establishment figures have led double lives, actually believing in the opposite of what they appear to be supporting. Some of these people have been spies who have passed secrets to other countries whose ideals they have believed in; for example, the supposedly more equal society of Soviet Russia.

Write a radio play in which a top civil servant, who has been secretly sabotaging the aims of his or her bosses, has a conversation with his or her partner, another relative, and finally an interrogator from the police. You will have to decide how the final interview will end.

Assignment 4

Caryl Churchill might have written a further speech in this play in which Barbara responds to her sister's revelation about the Judge in an equally long speech.

Write Barbara's reply to Caroline's statement.

Critical response

Assignment 1

Caryl Churchill has decided to begin this television play with what might have been its climax: the murder of the Judge. She also reminds viewers, at other points in the play, of the killing of its central character.

What is the effect of this technique? How does it influence your thinking about the Judge each time you see it? How does the repetition of the killing influence your feelings about the ending of the play? Discuss this with a friend. Make notes on each of these questions after discussion.

Plan an essay evaluating the use of visual repetition of the images of murder in the play.

Assignment 2

This play has been written to provoke audience reaction in various ways. List the moments in the play that seem to demand a definite response, or to make you wonder about the author's intentions. For each moment on your list, name the technique used, considering the following:
- visual images
- dialogue
- action

- timing
- dramatic structure
- character interaction.

If this play is intended to provoke thinking in the audience, how successful has it been? What are your own thoughts about each of the moments on your list? Note them down, and then compare notes with a partner.

Now plan and write an essay discussing how successful you think this play has been in challenging you into reactions and reflecting on them.

Coursework assignments on more than one play

Assignment 1

Make a chart using the headings below to help you decide which plays deal with similar themes. Under each heading write the name(s) of the play(s), adding to the chart any more themes you can think of which are not mentioned here:
- coping with the unexpected
- different attitudes towards society
- loyalty
- disappointment
- the future
- the capacities of 'ordinary' women
- female–male relationships
- the 'supporting' roles of women.

Now write an essay comparing Caryl Churchill's development of one of these themes in two or three plays.

Begin by re-reading your Reading log for notes in which you have responded to your chosen theme. Then note down how the writer introduces and develops the theme in each play using dialogue, characterisation and dramatic effects. Decide what you think the writer is challenging the audience to consider through the theme.

Now plan your essay, noting the key quotations from the plays that you want to discuss in your essay. Try to show similarities and differences in the way the writer establishes and develops the theme. You will need to comment on what the writer has left the audience to consider at the end of each play, showing the techniques she has used to do this.

You should end your essay by saying how far you agree with what has been suggested to you by each play and what your own thoughts are about the issues raised by the theme.

Assignment 2

Compare the dramatic techniques (listed in Assignment 2 on page 77) of two or three plays, explaining your opinion of what effects they achieve.

Compare for example:
- the effect of the structure of scenes in *Seagulls* and *The Judge's Wife*
- the author's use of characters' ways of speaking in *Not Not Not Not Not Enough Oxygen* and *Seagulls*
- visual effects in *Seagulls* and *The Judge's Wife*
- setting up audience expectations to eventually surprise them in all three plays
- the very slow release of information to the audience in *Seagulls* and *Not Not Not Not Not Enough Oxygen*
- the endings of all three plays.

Assignment 3

Humour is used by Caryl Churchill for particular effects on the audience. Consider the uses of humour in two or three plays.

79

Assignment 4

Choose one of the three plays and form a group to prepare a performance, paying particular attention to the way you think the lines should be said.

Assignment 5

Write an introduction to these three plays for new readers.

Try to give an impression of what readers need to be prepared for. For example, what are the characteristics of Caryl Churchill's plays? Without giving too much away, say which play you have enjoyed most and why.

Assignment 6

Each of these plays has been written to be thought-provoking for the audience. Which do you feel has been most successful for you? What thoughts have been provoked by the play?

Write an imaginary conversation with the author developing your thoughts about one of the plays and imagining her responses.

Caryl Churchill replies to your thoughts in the way in which you think she would from the evidence of the plays and the interviews on pages vii–xiii in the Introduction to this book.

Assignment 7

You have been asked to turn one of these plays into a fable for a collection of stories that end in a (sometimes surprising) moral. These will be rather like the Chinese fable that gives *Seagulls* its name. Which play will you choose? Write the fable adding the moral on to the end in a final sentence beginning:

'Moral . . . . .' It does not have to be a moral you think Caryl Churchill intended. It might help to read your notes again on the plays' themes in your Reading log.

Assignment 8

Choose one statement by Caryl Churchill from the interviews in the Introduction on pages vii–xiii and discuss it in relation to one play. Begin by making notes on:
– why you have chosen this play
– what insights into the play come to you from thinking about the statement
– any ways in which the play develops the idea in the statement
– any aspect of the play which contradicts the statement.

Wider reading

This is a selection of plays by or about women. You may need some help from your teacher in choosing wider reading from this list.

New plays for young people

Each of the following collections contains at least one play by a woman playwright. They are all edited by Rony Robinson and published by Hodder and Stoughton:

Ask Me Out
They Said You Were Too Young
None of Them Knew Why I Was Crying
You Don't Know You're Born

Collections including TV plays by women

Michael Church (ed.), *Intensive Care and Other TV Plays*, Longman Imprint.
Alison Leake (ed.), *A Special Occasion*, Longman Imprint.

Also intended for young people

Ian Lumsden (ed.), *Scriptz*, Unwin Hyman.

Other plays by or about women

Jane Arden, *Virgina Rex and the Gas Oven*, Calder and Boyars.
John Arden and Margaretta D'Arcy, *Vandalour's Folly*, Methuen.
Alan Ayckbourn, *Sisterly Feelings*, Longman Study Text.
Alan Ayckbourn, *A Woman in Mind*, Faber and Faber.
Aphra Benn, *The Rover*, Methuen.
Alan Bennett, *Talking Heads*, BBC Publications.
Bertolt Brecht, *The Caucasian Chalk Circle*, Methuen.
———— *Mother Courage*, Methuen.
———— *The Good Woman of Szechwan*, Methuen.
Sarah Daniels, *Neaptide*, Methuen.
Shelagh Delany, *A Taste of Honey*, Methuen.
Maureen Duffy, *Rites*, Vintage.
Nell Dunn, *Steaming*, Amber Lane.
Pam Gems, *Piaf*, Penguin.
———— *Camille*, Penguin.
———— *Loving Women*, Penguin.
David Hare, *Slag*, Faber and Faber.
Ann Jellicoe, *The Sport of My Mad Mother*, Faber and Faber.
———— *The Knock*, Faber and Faber.
Doris Lessing, *Each His Own Wilderness*, Penguin.
———— *With a Tiger*, Davis-Poynter.

Liz Lockhead, *Mary Queen of Scots Got Her Head Chopped Off/Dracula*, Penguin.
Anthony Minghella, *Whale Music*, Methuen.
Mary O'Malley, *Once a Catholic*, Amber Lane.
Louise Page, *Golden Girls*, Methuen.
———— *Beauty and The Beast*, Methuen.
Willie Russell, *Educating Rita*, Longman Literature.
———— *Shirley Valentine*, Longman Literature.
———— *Stags and Hens*, Methuen.
George Bernard Shaw, *Pygmalion*, Longman Literature.
———— *Caesar and Cleopatra*, Longman Study Text.
———— *Major Barbara*, Longman Study Text.
———— *Saint Joan*, Longman Literature.
Sue Townsend, *The Secret Diary of Adrian Mole*, Methuen.
John Webster, *The Duchess of Malfi*, Longman Study Text.
Michelene Wandor, *Five Plays*, Playbooks/Journeyman.
Michelene Wandor (ed.), *Plays by Women I–IV*, Methuen.